_____

By

_____

On the Occasion of

_____

Date

_____

LIFE
After
DEATH

S.D. Gordon

*Updated in Today's Language
by Dan Harmon*

BARBOUR
PUBLISHING, INC.
Uhrichsville, OH

©MCMXCVIII by Barbour Publishing, Inc.

ISBN 1-57748-181-X

Published by Barbour Publishing, Inc.
P.O. Box 719
Uhrichsville, OH 44683
http://www.barbourbooks.com

Published in the United States of America.

LIFE
After
DEATH

Chapter 1

Death—Ceaseless Tragedy of Life

Commonplace But Always Sacred

It was almost four o'clock on a September morning. A strong young man walked slowly on a deserted street of a coastal city.

The gray was streaked with orange in the east as the new day pushed away the dying night's blackness. But he scarcely noticed it. He was absorbed with another conflict of light and night—in his spirit. His step was slow, his head bent. A dark mood gripped him. He was in the heavy daze of something very new to him.

He climbed the green hill where the city's water was stored. It overlooked the river beyond, with the wavy mass of green treetops nearer. He drew a little limp-covered Book from his pocket and sat down, reading the Book and looking up into the blue sky and out over the trees and the water

A few hours before, a life had slipped from his grasp. He had clung tenaciously. But softly, gradually, insistently, her spirit had gone. He was dazed with surprise and grief. It never had occurred to him she would die. He had held on with unyielding love until there was nothing left to hold onto. Only the breathless bit of a precious form remained.

The two had been as closely knit in spirit as two ever were, or could be. But now she was gone, beyond recall. That was clear. He was outwardly very quiet, attending to the things that needed doing. But within he gasped. He could not seem to get his breath. All life was changed. The world was a different place. She was gone. He was dazed, yet alert in spirit.

Now he sat still. The question asked itself: Where was she? The precious bit of flesh was there, tenderly cared for. But where was *she?* Not here. Somewhere. . . .Where?

The little Book seemed to open itself at John's dear old story of Jesus, and it seemed to stay open easily. A new, soft light shone from the old words. A quiet peace stole forth—a new peace, sweeter and more real, in the overwhelming daze that nearly swamped him. But a great, lonely feeling gripped his heart, mingling with the peace even while yielding to it.

He did not know how long he sat. Then he climbed slowly down the hill, back along the street they so often had walked together hand in hand.

The old house and the old routine were the same, but life was changed. It never could be the same again. He had entered the saddest experience of his life.

He has never forgotten it. Its memory clings as freshly as if it had happened yesterday.

The lights are all out
In the mansions of clay;
The curtains are drawn,
For the dweller's away;
She silently slipped
O'er the threshold by night,
To make her abode
In the city of light.

And how common! Common in its *frequency*—monotonously common. But at the same time sacred, a thing quite uncommon in its loneliness and grief, though it happens every hour of the day to someone.

Death is the most common thing in life. Its shadow never leaves. The mailman puts the notice in your box. The half-masted flag, the tolling church bell, the low requiem breathing out of church windows, the slow-moving procession of cars—these are things we encounter regularly. We pause briefly to honor someone gone, then continue our mad rush through life.

The old Book has barely begun before you hear Eve sobbing over her boy lying still. Almost at once you are in that striking chapter (Genesis 5) with its requiem of sorrow chanting monotonously, "and he died."

The despairing cries of a race going down beneath the great rush of waters and the wail of broken hearts in Egyptian homes over the dead firstborn catch your ears. If you hurry through the pages to get away, you encounter the dear old Singer of Israel sobbing his heart out over his handsome, self-willed son.

And the newer pages open with the cries of the brokenhearted mothers of Bethlehem. The symphony of sorrow seems unending.

Death Is Always a Tragedy

Death is always a tragedy to somebody. Life is tragic. Death seems to be the dark double knot on the end of the tragic thread of life. No day passes without death breaking someone's heart. No shelter is dry from the dripping rain of death's tear.

Homes are broken. The dear family circle is scattered beyond reunion. Habits of a lifetime are snapped. Plans and ambitions are thrown to the mocking winds. Memory trails its minor chords along every street and hallway of the bruised heart and disrupted life.

The world's wars have added a terrible emphasis to all this. There is a terrific uncertainty in most minds and hearts. This uncertainty becomes the worst pain of all.

The questions troop in insistently, day and night, demanding answers. "Is he still alive?" "Is there a spirit world?" "Is there really something beyond this life?" "Where has he gone?" "How are things with him now?"

East and west, south and north, in primitive village and cultured home, among so-called heathens and in the floodlight of truth, human hearts cry out: *"Where has he gone?"* Sorrow unites the races. Differences, hatreds, and prejudices are submerged in the hour of common sorrow.

Yet there is a clear light. There is an answer to these questions. There is certainty. There is positive, dependable information. It is enough to give a golden tint to every black cloud. There is another melody that overcomes minor chords in the symphony of sorrow.

We want to talk a bit now of that certainty. We want to find the keynote of the mingled symphony where joy sweetens sorrow and sets your hearts singing and tingling while waiting for the reunion day.

Fierce was the wild billow,
  Dark was the night,
Oars labour'd heavily,
  Foam glimmer'd white,
Trembled the mariners,
  Peril was nigh;
Then saith the God of God,
  "Peace! It is I!"

Ridge of the mountain wave,
  Lower thy crest,
Wail of Euroclydon,
  Be thou at rest.
Sorrow can never be,
  Darkness must fly,
When saith the Light of Light,
  "Peace! It is I!"

Jesu, deliverer,
  Come Thou to me,
Soothe Thou my voyaging
  Over life's sea;
Thou when the storm of Death,
  Roars sweeping by,
Whisper, O Truth of Truth,
  "Peace! It is I!"

— Hymn of St. Antolius

Chapter 2

What Can We Know About Those Who Have Died?

The Oldest Question

Where is he? We see that narrow box and slender mound of flower-adorned earth. But *he* is not *there* —or *is* he? *He*—where is *he?*

It is the oldest question. It has been wrung from every generation by grief as those left behind stare over the grave, into the gray beyond.

Our earliest mother knelt brokenhearted beside the body of her boy. It was a triple grief, for her. Her boy was dead—grief enough. He died through passionate violence and, worse yet, violence by his own brother.

Grief was born in a mother's broken heart. But grief's original birthplace was in the heart of God, when His prodigal world went away from the old fireside. His was a mother-heart—a father-mother heart. A broken heart. God's heart is a human heart, and more. We get our human hearts from His human heart; we are made in His likeness.

The question and the grief have never quit, since that day just outside the Eden gate. Grief is ceaseless. It has occurred in every time and place. And the question stabs into the most sacred hour and corner.

The Greeks were masters of their known world. Their sense of beauty has never been surpassed.

17

Their chiseled marble, clean architecture and noble teachings set the world's standard. But their answer to this old question could not stop the grief in their own broken hearts.

He was gone, they said. It was the end. There was nothing beyond. At least, this is what their brains said, though their hearts never accepted the answer. There was a sharp break between brain and heart, never bridged by their philosophy.

Other Greeks disagreed. But the best they could imagine was a cheerless, aimless, colorless, unappealing existence after death. That was the best answer the best Greek wisdom and culture could offer.

The Romans were masters of sheer, brutal force, organized with rarest skill. They overpowered the Greeks, but they could not master this question. It forced them to admit themselves mastered, outdone in the presence of grief. They followed the same path cut by Greek philosophy. They had no light to relieve the gray gloom.

The earlier dwellers of the Nile saw no better light. They could pierce the sky with their pyramids. But their longing, tear-dimmed eyes could not pierce past the grave. The Euphrates' sages stopped dumb at the same place, hoping, wishing, wondering, but skeptical. The Phoenicians could shape an alphabet to be carried through one national culture after another, up to our own English language. But they could not shape a teaching about the future that could ease the heart tug at the grave.

Modern-day teachers following the same path of reasoned research have nothing to add to the earlier thinking. The best they can suggest is a vague uncertainty. They are wearisome comforters, like Job's friends. They say the candle is snuffed out. He is gone for good. It is the end. *Or,* you dimly can see him wandering aimlessly about in a gray gloom that only adds a touch of bitterness to the grief.

It is a cheerless answer. The cold light of reason is well called "cold." This is the best and most its lantern can do in the night of human sorrow.

But stop. That is not all. There is another answer, and it is the answer of answers. There is no begging of the question here. It stands in sharp contrast to the other answers. They are vague; it is positive and clear. There is an element of thoughtful, measured certainty that begins to ease the heart at once.

Indeed, certainty is a marked characteristic of this answer. The certainty is startling and refreshing. The sky clears. Sunlight begins to edge the clouds with its cheery, golden glint.

A Small Group of Facts

A small group of facts underlie our certainty about the life after death. A fact is something that is really so. It stands in direct contrast to theory, speculation, logic, or argument. A fact is a real state of things. It is practical. It is something you can put your finger on and say, "This is so."

The sun is a fact. You look up and see it. There it is. The theorist explains that you really don't see the sun, for it is more than 90 million miles away and the human eye cannot see that far; it is a reflection you see. But the average, busy person is impatient with theory. He or she says, "There is the sun in plain sight. You can see it. You feel its heat. You work by its light." And that settles it. We go on about our work. The sun is a potent fact in common life.

To the plain person on the street, too busy for fine theory, a small group of facts about death are visible as plainly as the sun in the sky. One's daily life can be shaped by these facts as truly as by the light and heat of the sun.

First, *Christian civilization is a fact.* It is very different from the civilization of the Caesars, which covered the known world in the time of Christ.

Treatment of the weak is the acid test of any civilization. In those years there was slavery, both black and white. Now there is not only freedom from slavery but the highest civil rights for the humblest person, and state education for everyone, rich or poor. Back then a woman was a chattel, merely a piece of property. Now she is loved, shielded, cultured, queen of the home and more. In those times children were sometimes despised and neglected, even killed. Now they are prized and cared for as our most precious possessions.

In Roman times superstition guided the care of the sick and the mentally deficient (or they were ignored). Now science and humanitarianism combine their best, caring even for those who cannot pay for it. In those days the most sordid, cold selfishness was normal. Now billions of dollars are given voluntarily for the relief of the needy. Back then there were no commonly accepted standards of morality; sexual morality was regulated by property rights or ownership (as is so even today in some non-Christian cultures). Now there is a moral standard which, though continually violated, is recognized and influences common life.

Take these few items as threads in a fabric. It is impossible to state the case fully in a few words.

For Christian civilization is an atmosphere that fills the lungs. We are too much part of it to sense it fully. Only an ancient Roman, if dropped down into it, could appreciate the tremendous contrast as he tried to catch his startled breath.

The difference is stupendous. These and similar criteria are recognized as the distinctive traits of Christian civilization. The contrast between Christian and non-Christian societies is painful *and* is a living exposition of Christian civilization.

The question has been raised of whether Christian civilization is merely a veneer, a pretense covering something that needs hiding. This suspicion seems to have grown like a tree, where scavenger birds find their nests in its protecting branches, preying on humankind.

But Christian civilization is not an original thing. It has no independent life, no roots of its own. It is an outgrowth of something else. And that something else is greater than the outgrowth. The root is more than the shoot growing out of it—much more.

If a savage war swept over the world and wiped out all Christian civilization, the root would remain as full of life and fertility as before. It would put forth new shoots. And its growth again would largely cover the earth.

Christianity Is a Fact

This leads to the second fact: *Christianity is a fact.* Christian civilization is an outgrowth of Christianity. Christianity is the root. Christian civilization is the shoot; it has no separate life of its own. Furthermore, it seems pretty plain that Christian civilization isn't the chief outgrowth.

These radical differences between two civilizations really must be classed as *incidentals*. They are blessedly revolutionary but are mere by-products. Christian civilization is a by-product, nothing more. It is a by-product of Christianity. It is not the main thing itself.

By common consent, no nation today is Christian in the profession and daily practices of most of its people. Government policies, while taking on the outer coloring of Christian civilization, are the reverse of Christianity underneath, dominated by a selfish, grasping spirit. Christianity has not had the opportunity to produce its chief result in the generic life of Christian nations.

So if these distinctive traits of Christian civilization are mere incidentals or by-products of

23

something else, that something else must be not only a fact, but a fact of immensely deeper significance.

Christianity is an *ideal,* a *group of moral principles,* and a vital *power* that makes the ideal and principles real in human life. It radically can change a human life from bad to good. And it *does* this. It presents a high ideal, makes a person long for it intensely, and then makes it an actual experience in that person's life, overcoming the most stubborn opposition.

No stronger statement could be made of any power. It changes the human will at its core, and it does this wholly from within. No other known power has done that or can do it.

The drunkard becomes sober and hates the evil he or she once loved so passionately. The impure becomes pure, the thief honest, the covetous generous, the wavering and drifting purposeful, the weak strong. And the changed person becomes a new factor influencing his or her surroundings.

Every continent, civilization, and distinct race has living evidence of such change. Yellow men and brown, black men and white, all have revealed this unmatched, solitary power at work.

The extremes meet here. The city slum and the savage tribe both acknowledge this transforming power.

This is what I mean when I say Christian civilization is merely incidental to Christianity. The radical changing of human character from bad to good—this is the chief thing. *Anything* else is incidental. The civilization is superficial. This goes to the very core. Indeed, this is the starting point of a true, abiding civilization.

So Christianity is seen to be a fact, plainly evident. It is an indisputable fact even to those who hate it.

Christ Is a Fact

But there is another step. Put your foot on the next rung of the ladder. Christianity leads you straight to something else. And again, it is something greater than itself. The something else proves to be Someone else. For Christianity is not a thing or a system in itself. It is merely a shoot growing from a root.

As Christian civilization is rooted in Christianity, Christianity is rooted in Christ. It comes from Him. The two are inseparable. And the shoot is less than the root.

Cannon Liddon once said, "Christianity is Christ." That means Christianity can be understood only as one draws to Christ. He is its standard. So we have the third fact: *Christ is a fact.*

I am ignoring a lot of evidence here. I am talking for the busy reader on the move, whose attention must be caught by plain talk if it is to be caught at all. At this simple level, where all must confess what their eyes see, Christian civilization certifies the fact of Christianity. And the fact of Christianity certifies the fact of Christ.

Christ stands not just for those thirty-three years of His personality. He stands for the powerful influences that radiated and still radiate from that personality and from those years filled with tremendous happenings.

The name *Christ* stands for ideals—the highest ideals known. It stands for ideals lived—actually lived—amid the stress of our common life. It stands for love and sacrifice beyond the love and sacrifice of anyone else. It stands for power in overcoming immorality, prejudice, superstition, hatred, and the deadliest evil. It stands for power in completely overcoming death itself and living a new, triumphant life on earth past the grave.

Christ stands for even more—the power that can make that ideal a living reality in human life today.

For what has been said of Christianity must be said of Christ. He is the power of Christianity. Christ is Christianity—the real thing. And He is more than that, for all the power of Christianity comes from Him. Christ is a fact, a tremendous, unmistakable, unchangeable fact.

The evidence is plain and open. A glance at the dateline in the morning paper and the postmark of the last letter you received tells of the fact of Christ. Contact with someone you know who lives the real Christian life and has been blessedly changed makes that fact take hold of your very heart.

But another egg is in this nest. The fact of Christ is linked to another fact: the Christ-Book. The Bible is a fact, tied to the fact of Christ. The two are inextricably interwoven, for Christ is the very heart-blood of this Book. You simply *cannot* take Him out of it! To do so would be to take the Book out of itself.

It is striking that you must go to this Book for the essential facts about Christ Himself. The Book is the one original source of information about Him. The Book that tells firsthand about the divine Christ must itself be divine. It is a lonely Book, quite by itself in its standards, ideals, and power. It would take a Christ to make a Christ, and it would take a Christ to make this Christ-Book.

Inspired Revelation Is a Fact

The Bible is a fact. I do not just mean it is a fact that there is such a book. This Book is a living fact or factor in Christian civilization, in Christianity, in Christian teaching among non-Christian people, in the personal history of Christ Himself and in the human lives it has touched and molded.

Wherever it is known, the Bible is accepted as the one standard of moral teaching unlike any other. By common consent, its contributions to law, politics, moral philosophy, business ethics, and sanitation are the underlying foundations of all books written on these subjects. The Bible is characterized by a fine reserve, a conservative caution and a rare modesty about itself. Its high moral character is freely accepted wherever it is known.

The Bible has been unmatched throughout history in its ideals of life; in its originality; in its unfailing freshness and adaptation after centuries; in its subtle, real touch through the human medium by something more than human; and in its one outstanding Person, Christ. The Bible is a fact in the life of the race.

And there is another hatch in this brood. Notice a striking thing: This conservative Book actually claims to be a distinctive revelation from God Himself. It claims to be so filled with the Holy Spirit that we can depend on it as a revelation of God's will, purposes, and plan. And it is so interwoven with these other plain facts that by accepting them we accept the Bible and its claim.

So very quietly, a fifth fact adds itself to the group: *It is a fact that there is a revelation from God.* I know this is disputed vigorously and bitterly. Indeed, the spirit of bitterness and tenacity in the propaganda against this fact is distinctively scholarly. This spirit suggests the real source behind the dispute. There is a bitter hatred, a serpentine quality of subtlety and venom.

The point is this: The fact that there is a revelation from God is as clear as the previous four facts. It is as clear as the fact of the sun overhead.

You may rest in knowing the acceptance of these facts is in full accord with the most rugged intellectual integrity. Merely as a *matter of evidence,* regardless of the moral consequences, this group of facts safely may be left to the verdict of the highest courts.

Muddy Vs. Real Scholarship

I have put the matter in this simple, direct, positive way because of the muddy scholarship we hear today. (That is, it passes for scholarship—and it certainly is muddy. It is marked by the absence of clear, vigorous thinking and dialog.)

A system of instruction has grown up that uses the fine old name of scholarship. It sits in high places, in universities and divinity schools. Its text-books and influences are found in grade schools. Its dominant tactic is to raise questions and leave them hanging in the air. With elaborate speculation, it plants doubt, and this doubt spreads among the hearers.

Using scholarly language, this system breathes a gray, foggy atmosphere. The facts that would counteract its theories are ignored, minimized, or misconstrued.

It is common for young people trained in Christian homes and old-fashioned Christian truth to catch these germs of doubt. The disease becomes chronic, and the moral fiber soon breaks down.

We should be grateful for true scholarship. The

best scholarship of all time was headed by one who may be called the greatest of all scholars. His scholarly research led him to accept a direct, distinct revelation from God.

He was taught in the Egyptian schools—the world's universities of that day. And he had that rare instinct for independent research regardless of where it leads—the mark of true scholarly genius. He pursued the original sources like no one else. After his Egyptian "university" work and long postgraduate study at the University of the Desert came two intensive postgraduate courses, six weeks each, *on Horeb*. (That, indeed, was going to the original sources.)

Real scholarship's results are close at hand in every standard library, if you want the facts. And nothing is more easily settled than the utter dependability of this Book and the essential accuracy of its transmission to us. We have the Book's message as it came from God to and through its writers under the holy spell of God's Spirit.

That there is a revelation from God is a fact. That fine word *revelation* is used here in its old-fashioned, full meaning. It is not watered down. It is a revelation of something that could have been obtained in no other way. It is reasonable. In fact, it takes reason to a higher level. Reason, with its marvelous, godlike powers, slowly works its way up to certain conclusions, and then must stop. It can go no further. This revelation tells what reason cannot find out because of natural limitations.

Furthermore, this revelation is in full accord with the moral character of the Book that contains it. It is in perfect accord with the character of God and Christ. It is the kind of revelation you would expect from such a source. In this way it stands in sharp contrast to other literature dealing with such matters.

The Practical Bible

It is remarkable that the Book of God deals with the questions that have puzzled every generation. It fully answers the question *"Where is he?"* It brings the comfort of certain knowledge to the bruised, torn heart.

It deals with the questions war asks again—questions about the spirit world, of which our world is only a part, about life beyond the grave, about communication with the dead. In short, it begins where reason ends. It answers these questions with startling certainty, not mere human philosophizing. It brings us a great sense of relief, refreshment, and real comfort and strength.

The more you surrender to the mastery of the Lord Jesus, the keener and more disciplined you grow in your mental processes. The more sensitive you become to the presence and will of the Holy Spirit within you, the more your inner spirit answers to the living Spirit within this Book. And the surer your spirit becomes of God and of the spirit world.

We now turn to this solitary Book of God and ask the tense old question: *"Where is he?"* At once your whole outlook changes, as if you are stepping from the night into a house flooded with light. Outside, you grope in darkness or twilight; God is hard to see. Here, God is admitted, and the whole equation changes.

The personal equation—that is, the God equation—completely alters the problem and its solution. What is impossible without God becomes the natural thing with God. It seems so natural now that you know instinctively in your spirit that *God belongs in you.*

We find at once that this is a Book of thoughtful distinctions. It does not slur over moral matters. It clearly distinguishes between individuals, based on their heartfelt attitudes toward God and good.

So the answer to the question is in two parts. The second part is the painful part of the answer; that will come in our next discussion. Right now we want to talk about the first part of the answer. What do we know for sure about those *in touch of heart with God* who have died?

Our Question Answered

I think it may be clearer if I begin with a simple, running story of what happens to these people at death, without using references. Then we will gather the great teaching passages from the Book, citing chapter and verse, and then compile certain outstanding events from the Book that illustrate and emphasize the teachings. The story grows entirely out of these teachings and events.

Where is he? You may want to find a corner where you can think quietly and try to *take in* the wondrous story that answers the question.

The moment of death has come. The doctor, standing still with a trained finger on the pulse, says in a hushed voice, "He is gone." *Where?* The beginning of death is the beginning of life. The closing here is the opening there. The end is really the beginning. The shutting door to us is an opening door to *him*.

Quicker than you can bat your eye or catch your breath, he is consciously in the immediate presence of our glorified Lord Jesus Christ. He does not go alone. A convoy of bright-faced angels meet him and take his spirit straight up into the presence of Christ in the Homeland.

He does not travel a long distance through space; he is instantly at his new destination. Time and space and distance belong to our thinking down here. It takes a certain length of time, we say, to travel a certain distance. That is necessary earth talk. Up there, in the spirit world, they go as swiftly as thought through what we would call a long distance. We cannot possibly take it in, but it clearly is so.

And so the moment he is gone from us, he arrives in the new Home. He sees Jesus. He meets loved ones gone before. There is a wondrous reunion *at once*. He hears music unlike human ears have ever heard. All pain, all mental stress, all spiritual strain are gone. He is at Home in a new world where life and light, harmony and joy, are the very atmosphere, to an extent we cannot understand down here. His cup of enjoyment and happiness is full.

That is the essence of what happens to him the instant he slips the tether of earthly life. Now, we may be just as sure of certain intensely interesting details.

He is the same person we knew down here. His *identity* is unchanged and undisturbed. The same essential characteristics familiar to his loved ones remain. All the traits that make up his individuality remain the same, though the bad or weak moral traits are gone. The identity of the person we knew here will persist through all the growth and development to come.

Closely related is the matter of *mutual recognition*. We often wonder if we will know each other up there. Nothing is more certain than the promise of instant, full, mutual recognition. Our powers over there will be keener and better developed.

But, you think, with the passage of years, those of us left behind on earth change—perhaps radically. And the dead change, too, do they not? It's painful to think we won't instantly recognize the one we loved so intimately.

A mother may be thinking of her child who died in infancy. Though years have passed, she probably still thinks of the child as a little babe. Yet she would be grieved beyond words to find her child, after years of separation, still tiny and undeveloped.

A little thought reveals the comforting truth. Over there, in His presence, is fullness of life. Our spiritual perception will be far keener there than here. Our loved ones will have *grown,* and during that growth all that is best will have developed with the individual's distinctive traits. The mother, crossing the threshold of life, will recognize instinctively that her babe has grown and matured into a cultured, poised being. The mother will desire intensely to have it so. She immediately will recognize that this thoughtful, mature man or woman who has grown into the fine spiritual image of Christ is her child of long years ago. And with recognition will come great joy because of the growth. The recognition will be instant, mutual, and joyous.

Furthermore, as he comes into Christ's presence, there will be *no discussion of his sin.* This man we are talking about is in heartfelt touch with the Father, and the sin question has been settled for him. Christ's death and resurrection settled it. The blood of Christ covers his sin, and he is accepted by the Father even as His only begotten Son is accepted. He begins to appreciate just what a tremendous thing Jesus did for him in dying.

But he will show *certain moral changes.* As he comes into Christ's presence, certain things in his character will be removed or altered, just as putting a lump of gold ore into the fire instantly separates whatever is in the ore that is not gold; the other part is burned or discarded.

Christ is pictured as a Man of Fire. Fire purifies. Fire consumes what cannot stand its flame. Christ's mere presence will act on the mortal's character, just as the fire acts on the lump of gold ore.

Whatever in a human's character (described by Paul as "wood, hay, and stubble") won't stand the fire of the pure presence of Jesus will be removed, as by fire. Selfishness, pettiness, uncontrolled passion, self-will, bitterness, narrowness, the artificial —all will go.

In some cases the fire may burn up more than it leaves, for fire is relentlessly truthful. No doubt many a human's earthly life will be practically lost because it has been controlled by un-Christlike motives. But the soul, or afterlife, will be saved, for that is a matter of Christ's blood. Indeed, some will be saved because of what the fire does. Not even Christ's blood will save the growth of selfishness encrusting the person who at heart really does trust Christ. The blood saves the person; the fire burns up the bad growths. There will be some pretty severe shrinkage in the presence of the purifying Man of Fire.

The Changed Outlook

The *whole outlook* changes up there. It will be like climbing a high mountain, above the clouds, after living down here in the foggy, misty valley. We will know fully, then, just as we are known fully now. The point of view will change completely. Our sense of values will change instantly—both shrinking and growing.

Everything is seen up there at its real value—as God values it. Some things we cling to desperately will be acknowledged as worthless. And things we dimly recognize as good but let slip, or hold loosely, will be seen as pure gold. We will see clearly, even as God now sees clearly. There will be a radical shift in values of earthly things—controlling motives, corporate and government policies, suffering, common problems. This change will be revolutionary. It will come to many with unspeakable shock, but it will be recognized at once that things at last are seen at their true values.

The new outlook will affect our understanding of *our loved ones still living down on earth*. We will be fully conscious of things on earth. But we will see all things from God's viewpoint. We will understand much of God's general plans for the future. We will sense how things will turn out.

If you are wondering how we can see our earthly loved ones' difficulties and pain without being disturbed, remember we will be seeing it all from God's standpoint. There will be an utter change in our evaluation of these things. We will be content in the knowledge of God's tender love.

Also remember our loved ones already up there in the Homeland *are growing*. We know this by simple inference. Growth is a law of life, and up there they have real life. Whatever has God's touch on it grows—and up there is God's own fireside. All things are His way, so there is growth of the finest, truest kind.

The dear, tiny babies who have gone through the upper doorway have been growing. Like the child Jesus, they have grown in wisdom, in stature, and in favor with God and men. That includes mental, spiritual, and social growth. Under the touch of God's creative power, ever at work, and under the tutelage of the angels, they have grown in maturity and poise. They have grown in every way that makes perfect human character. For Heaven is a school as well as a home—although the words "school" and "home" both mean something much finer there. All the training of perfect school life and all the wonderfulness of a fine home life are blessedly commonplace up there.

Heaven has been preached and taught and hymned out of touch with true human feelings and thought. I recall distinctly a few lines of a hymn I sang in my youth:

Where congregations ne'er break up,
And sabbaths have no end.

The melody was a fine one, and I loved it. I still sing it. The tune has kept the words in my memory.

But when I thought about it as a boy, it didn't awaken any special enthusiasm about going to Heaven. The sabbaths I knew had unnatural restraints (though I think those restraints that irked me were decidedly better than today's looseness). I had a youthful vision of Heaven as one ceaseless church service on plain, hard, wooden benches with straight, stiff backs; psalms and hymns; long, proper sermons. I think many others have a similar idea about the other life.

But it is God's real home up there. Things are as He plans. God is rhythmic and purposeful, so there is a purpose, motive, and definite aim in each life. There is work toward a goal and the zest of seeing

41

things grow. That is part of true life.

Each one up there has a task and occupation—and a rare joy in doing it. It is a busy, purposeful, active life, but without worry, crowding, drudgery, or hurtful competition.

Service According to Ability

There is something else to be said emphatically, but gently. Emphatically, because we rarely talk about it; gently, because it touches a sore spot in our Christian life.

It is this: Your occupation up there, your privilege of serving the King personally, will be *according to ability*. But "ability" has a new meaning. It refers to the *spirit traits* that are grown down here.

If you are being true to the Lord Jesus in the stress of life, you are growing certain character traits. You are cultivating an inner spiritual life that is coloring and shaping your outer life. In obeying the Lord fully, you experience difficulties on earth. You encounter opposition and persecution, sometimes subtle and deep.

You are growing a spiritual sensitivity to the Master's presence, voice, and way of doing things. You are growing, unconsciously, the traits you'll need in the Master's upper service. Your vision is being cleared, your ear trained to hear His voice, your spirit sharpened to understand, your judgment disciplined, your mood made like His, responsive to Him and to those similarly in touch with Him.

Let me say gently that it is pathetic how many people are concerned only that they will be saved. The thought of serving the Master *after* being saved is not considered. The concern for personal salvation is natural, but many of us seem to believe once we've settled the matter of salvation, like taking out an insurance policy, we are free to go on living our selfish, worldly way, like the outer crowd. The motives of the world are largely our motives. We don't see much difference.

The point of stress if this: Our life there, our privilege of serving the King, will be based on our Christian lives here. It will be an outstanding honor to run errands, carry out commissions, and be entrusted with other forms of service.

And mark it well: *Anyone may serve* up there who is willing. No favoritism will be shown. Of course, honored errands will be assigned only to those who *can* perform them, those who have developed the required character traits.

It seems quite clear that when our Lord Jesus comes again to heal the earth's hurt, He will be accompanied not by everyone who is saved through His blood, but by those saved ones who are "*chosen and faithful*." They will be the ones who, in their lives on earth, have answered the *call* to personal salvation. They have been *chosen* for a particular service *and* they have been *faithful* to their Lord in doing what He asked.

This will be the simple law of service up in the Homeland and in the coming kingdom. The King's errands will be entrusted to those who have grown the necessary traits. And those traits are grown in our earthly life by following fully our blessed Lord Jesus.

Yet note carefully that every cup of happiness will be full up there. There will be different sorts of cups, different sizes, but each will be as full as it will hold. We will be absorbed with our glorious King. There will be the sweetest fellowship and fullest unity. But some will be honored in service while others cannot be—and the justice of this will be acknowledged readily by everyone.

It appears a lot of people will be saved by the skin of their teeth, in Job's words. They are in, but barely in; saved, but barely saved. Christ not only had to die to get them saved, but has to burn off a lot of stuff accumulated down here that can't go through the door up there.

This seems to be the simple picture drawn for us in this Book of God. There is much local color to add, but this answers the age-old question about our loved ones who have died, whose hearts are in touch with God.

Now Turn to the Book

Now we want to turn to the Book directly for *the detailed study* from which this simple picture is drawn. The old Hebrew Scriptures, the Old Testament, are flooded with *the kingdom concept.* The constant preoccupation of these writers is not death and Heaven and the life beyond, but a new condition coming on the earth.

A King is coming, and through Him a kingdom. The kingdom the authors are thinking about will be on earth. The triumph of right on the earth is their predominant thought. This outlook is based distinctly on God's promises to Abraham, David, and the other fathers of their people.

It is really the same as with the writers of the New Testament, where the dominant thought is of Someone coming back to earth, to right all wrongs and restore Eden on the earth.

This view makes the references to the future life stand out. Indeed, the indication is that these old writers didn't discuss the future life much; *they took it for granted.* This is the setting of the passages we want to study.

Other things are taken for granted, too. *God is taken for granted.* He is above death. We are his creatures, breath of His own breath. We have the same quality of life as He. We have been hurt badly by sin. As a result, there is death for the body. But the life within us is of the same essential sort as God's life. We share his quality of life, through His gracious, creative touch.

The other world is taken for granted. There *is* another world, a bigger part of the world we are in. It is another sort of world, the part we do not see. God's home and fireside are there. There is no death there, for God talks to successive generations. Humans come and go on earth, but God is continuous. It is like the harvests coming and going, with the farmer continuing season after season. This is the common point of view throughout the Book.

And God is concerned directly about things here. The scriptural authors write countless times, "And God said." Jacob is awed by God speaking to him at Jabbok, but it never occurs to him to question it. Abraham's heart is stilled when God appears in a dream or vision, and he accepts it as something by which to form his plans.

Death is taken for granted, as a dreaded passage to something beyond. It is something unnatural, a break. It is like passing through a dark, gloomy valley on your way to the mountaintop. This is revealed incidentally in the language used.

For instance, death commonly is called *sleep.* Sleep is temporary and is followed by waking. There is no direct analogy to death in nature. Winter is not death, but sleep. Spring is the waking season, with the powers refreshed. The grain of wheat is said to "die"—but this is a natural step toward the coming harvest. The death stage of humans is *unnatural,* a sharp rupture in nature's order.

In the Book, kings are said to be sleeping with their fathers. Jacob says, "When I sleep with my fathers." David cries out joyously, "I shall be satisfied *when I awake,* with thy likeness" (Psalm 17:15). This is as common in the Old Testament as in the clear resurrection light of the New.

This comparison of sleep with death is unique to

the Bible. It seems to have *originated* there. Its use elsewhere seems to imitate this old Biblical use.

Incidental Teachings

A group of *incidental teachings* touch the subject indirectly. Incidental evidence is always strong evidence, like Ehud's left-handed thrust (Judges 3). It reveals an atmosphere, attitude, outlook that immediately defines the dominating faith. Look at a few of these incidental teachings.

In the creation story, it is said God breathed into man's nostrils the breath of life. God earlier had created the lower animals. Man's creation is distinctly additional. God's own breath was breathed into man. Man is of God's essence, *creatively*. We are like God in the possession of life, the fact of life, and the sort of life. This is creative. It is not redemptive action. The creative, sustaining, preserving power of God continues despite sin. It is part of God's love.

In the outstanding passage, Isaiah 53, is a significant incidental statement: "When thou hast made his soul a sin-offering [put to death] he shall see his seed, he shall prolong his days." This is repeated a few lines later. Because he has poured out his soul unto death, "therefore will I divide him a portion with the great," etc. Here is not only life after death but a victorious life after a peculiarly humiliating death (Isaiah 53:10–12). It indicates continued life after death has lost control.

In the remarkable last chapter of Daniel is a clear teaching of a coming resurrection. It directly implies continued life of the spirit while the body mingles with dust. "Many of them that sleep in the dust of the earth shall awake; these [that awake] to everlasting life; the others [that do not awake at this time] shall be to shame and everlasting abhorrence" (Daniel 12:2, in Tregelles's translation).

A personal remark to Daniel closes the chapter: "Thou shalt rest, and shalt stand in thy lot at the end of the days." Paraphrased: "Thou shalt die, but when these events occur thou shalt be living and be in thine allotted place" (Daniel 12:13).

The large group of teachings about the resurrection become invaluable indirect evidence. Clearly, if there is a resurrection, it is based on a continuation of the human spirit whose body lies in the grave. The resurrection involves continued individual identity, for each spirit reenters its own body. The resurrection presumes there is a spirit world, all the deceased whose hearts are in touch with God are in His immediate presence, and His irresistible power overcomes the power of death.

All references to Christ's second coming belong in this group of incidental teachings. Whatever view we may hold about it today is immaterial, for the moment. Clearly, in the Book is a living faith in His return. His appearance was expected in that generation.

These references express a belief in an unseen spirit world, where Christ lived in the same body the disciples saw and touched after His resurrection. Those who had died and were in touch with Him were in that spirit world. They would return with Him in great victory and gladness.

Note Jesus' constant standpoint: He had come down from His Father's immediate presence on an errand to the earth. When the errand was done He would go back home again. That made the spirit world a very real thing to Him. The phrase "eternal life," which originated with Jesus and the Gospels, carries with it the same significance.

When the lame man was healed at the beautiful gate of the temple, Peter said of Jesus, "Whom the heavens must receive until the times of the restoration of all things, whereof God spoke by the mouth of his holy prophets" (Acts 3:21). There was clear teaching that Jesus, whom they had killed, was living then, up out of view, and that He would return to take control of things down here.

In his long teaching letter to the disciples in Rome, Paul made two incidental allusions full of suggestive meaning. The sufferings then being endured by some of Christ's followers were intense and real, but they were said to be insignificant when compared *"with the glory* which shall be *revealed to us-ward."*

In the same paragraph is a touching reference to the whole lower creation. It is said to be full of inarticulate groanings and intense birth pains, anticipating a coming new birth that would include all creation, including humankind (Romans 8:18, 22, 23). Not only is there life beyond death; it is a victorious life in which all wrongs are righted and the earth's hurt healed.

These are some of the indirect incidental teachings.

Outstanding Passages—Job

We come now to the *great teaching passages.* These are not selected, isolated texts, but are some of the mountain peaks.

Turn first to the book of Job. There is good reason to accept Job as the earliest written book of the Bible. If written by Moses, as is likely, it would reveal the conviction not only of Job the patriarch but of the scholarly Moses, who chose this incident for his remarkable essay on suffering. It reflects the common belief of the time, before the dimming of the creative floodlight.

Two outstanding passages come from Job's lips: "If a man die, shall he live again?" (Job 14:14) and "I know that my Redeemer liveth" (Job 19:25–27). These often-quoted verses at first seem to be contradictory. The first reference seems to express doubt—or at least, a question. The second rings with assurance.

The two really must be taken together. It seems quite clear they both were spoken within an hour's time, in the running conversation between the four men. As they talk, the cutting replies of his critics turn the sick man's mood so that the "Redeemer" passage seems to be a shift of emphasis, intensifying the question posed in the first passage. If you read the question ("If a man die, shall he live again?") in the context of their conversation, it plainly is not a doubt but rather an affirmation, a confession of Job's faith that he will live again.

Notice the *preceding* paragraph (Job 14:7–12) takes the lower view of things on earth. The tree dies and is gone. The man dies and, like the tree, is seen no more on earth. But in *this* paragraph containing the question (Job 14:13–17), the point of view clearly shifts. Here, Job is speaking to God in the upper, higher view.

> *Oh that thou wouldst hide me in the*
> *world of departed spirits.*
> *That thou wouldst keep me secret [hidden*
> *safety—as in Psalm 27:5] until thy*
> *wrath [in straightening out wrong] be*
> *past.*
> *That thou wouldst appoint me a set time,*
> *and [then] remember me!*
> *If a man die, shall he live? [I am so sure*
> *of it that]*
> *All the days of my present time of*
> *apprenticeship [or discipline] will I*
> *wait*
> *Till my release or graduation cometh.*
> *Thou wilt call [me up into thy presence],*
> *and I will answer thee [and come].*
> *Thou wouldst have a desire to [me], the*
> *work of thy [own] hand.*
> *But now [during this time of discipline*

> *on earth] thou numberest [or keepest*
> *a sharp count on] my steps.*

Job's statement seems confident in the final result after the present distress is over. A slight change in the order of the English would reflect Job's thought more accurately: "If a man die, he *shall* live again."

A little later in the passage, the mood of the conversation changes, and Job sees only the one side. With emphatic certainty, his voice rings out, "I *know* that my Redeemer liveth."

A glance at the connection (Job 19:13–19, 25) makes it plain that *my Redeemer* is contrasted with many other items. *My brethren, mine acquaintance, my kinsfolk, my familiar friends, my house, my maid, my servant, my wife, my children*—all have failed in some way. But my *Redeemer*, ah! I *know* about Him. He is unfailing.

That word *Redeemer* had a strong, tender, intimate meaning for Job and his listeners that we of a different culture miss. Job's Redeemer was his *goel,* his *nearest kinsman* who, because of a blood tie between them, would come to his help in any emergency. There was no closer family tie than with the *goel,* the vindicator, the blood brother.

Job is in the tightest corner of his life. His wealth, home, children, standing, and reputation all are gone—almost his life. At bay before these nagging pretender friends, he cries out, "Ah! I have a Kinsman. He is of my own family and I am of His. There is the tie of blood between us. He can cover all my needs, and He *will* do it. He is my Kinsman —redeemer. He will buy back all I've lost and make it good to me.

"He *liveth*. I don't see Him with these eyes, or feel Him, or hear His voice, but He *liveth*. *Liveth* in a perpetual, present tense. I will know death, but He knows only life. And He is my nearest Kinsman-redeemer. He will see that this death is overcome, and I will live with Him, my Kinsman.

"He will '*stand up*,' ready for action on my behalf, when the time for action comes. 'At last,' at the end of this troubled, earthly experience, He will stand up on behalf of me, His kinsman. Death will have done its worst.

"This body of mine, itching and tortured, scratched and weak, will be dust. But that is as far as death can go. It is the last of things here, but the first of things there. Life will be just beginning.

"Then, apart from my flesh, *I* shall see my Kinsman—redeemer, God. *I*, even *I*, will see Him. He will not be a stranger to me, but my nearest and dearest Kinsman." (See Job 19:25-27).

Note the truth taught here. There is continued

life beyond the grave for this man who is in touch of heart with God. It is life in the presence of God Himself, an intimate Friend and Kinsman. So it is a joyous life, with all hopes fulfilled. And there is continued identity: "*I, even I.*"

There is a righting of all earthly injustices. The quality of life beyond is the same as God's own life, for He and His redeemed ones are of the same family stock. They are kin. There is no closer tie than the family tie.

It is striking that in the dawn of this race, this clear teaching stands out so sharply. Even 1 Corinthians 15 is no more positive than this.

Other Old Testament Passages

Much later comes a striking episode in King Saul's time (1 Samuel 28:3–19). It is the story of the witch of Endor. This story, which we will discuss again later, is one of the two exceptional instances in the Bible of communication with those who have died.

For now, notice that Samuel, who had died, did

appear to the witch at Saul's request—to her intense
fright and astonishment (and regardless of her
witchery and pretended power). Samuel was recognized by Saul. He talked just as he always had
talked to Saul, giving the errant king another stinging rebuke. Samuel gave Saul precise, accurate
information about what would happen the next
day. There was no hidden meaning in his words.
He told of Saul's impending defeat, the loss of his
kingdom, and the death of Saul and his sons.

Samuel was living in the spirit world, and his identity was unmistakable. His knowledge of earthly
affairs was as keen as ever. His characteristics
were the same, his mind as sharp and his speech
as clear as before his death.

When David's child died, David said to his servants, "I will go to him, but he will not return to
me" (2 Samuel 12:23). Here is David's belief in the
continued existence of his child after death and the
expectation to be reunited. Furthermore, there is no
anticipation of communicating with the child during David's lifetime—an anticipation common
among the Israelites and the surrounding nations.
David stated plainly that the child would not return
to him here.

David's teaching in the Psalms is just as clear,
with a joyous tone throughout. Psalm 16 delights

in God's faithfulness. It summarizes the wonderful blessings of *the present life* for those who trust God wholly. It concludes (Psalm 16:9b–11):

> *[Even] my body also shall lie down in*
> *   the grave in confidence.*
> *For thou wilt not abandon, or forsake,*
> *   my soul in the world of departed*
> *   spirits;*
> *Neither wilt thou suffer thy holy one him-*
> *   self [thy beloved] to see [or go down*
> *   into] the pit.*
> *[Instead] thou, personally, wilt show me*
> *   the path of life [while my body awaits*
> *   in confidence the day of reunion]:*
> *In thy presence is fullness of joy;*
> *At thy right hand there are pleasures*
> *   forevermore.*

This nut is full of meat. Here is continued life after his body goes to the grave. It is a life of complete pleasure and enjoyment in the very presence of God. David believes the reward of joyous living is in the life to come. That life will be wonderfully more than the life here. It will include identity, recognition, and the fulfillment of all he has hoped for. He anticipates the resurrection of his body, reuniting with his spirit.

Psalm 17 voices the same assurance. David has been talking of the selfish, wicked ones who oppress him, who have all their good things in the present life. He closes (in Psalm 17:15):

> *As for me, I shall behold thy face in*
> *   righteousness.*
> *I shall be satisfied, when I awake, with*
> *   what I find thee to be when I am in*
> *   thy presence.*

Here, again, there is an afterlife. For David, it will be in God's presence. It fully satisfies the expectations of even David's vivid imagination.

Psalm 49, by one of Korah's sons, contrasts those who are in touch of heart with God and those who are not. It is a graphic picture (Psalm 49:15):

> *But God will redeem or vindicate my soul*
> *from the power of the world of departed*
> *spirits [at death]. That power will not get*
> *control over me. For He will receive me.*

Asaph likewise contrasts the wicked with the faithful (Psalm 73:24):

> *Thou wilt guide me with thy counsel [in the midst of the present difficult struggle], and afterward receive me to glory [or with glory].*

The same contrast comes in Psalm 140:13: "The upright shall dwell *in thy presence,*" while the wicked are cast into the fire.

In Ecclesiastes, we find Solomon writing at his lowest level, as a jaded cynic, dull with his passionate indulgences. But even here, he recognizes the afterlife: "Who knoweth the spirit of man that goeth *upward,* and the spirit of the beast that goeth *downward*" (Ecclesiastes 3:21). Both are alike, in earthly terms—both die and are gone. But one goes *up,* the other *down.* Again, "the dust [of the body] returns to the dust of the earth as it [originally] was, and *the spirit returneth to God who gave it*" (Ecclesiastes 12:7).

In the victorious climax over all Israel's enemies, Isaiah cries out, "He hath swallowed up death forever; and the Lord God will wipe away tears from off all faces" (Isaiah 25:8). On the surface, this looks forward to the coming kingdom on earth. But it also recognizes the changing character of death. Death will be put to death, and life will reign in its place. Paul's ringing cry of triumph over death in I

Corinthians 15:50–57 is based on this passage.

Notice also that Isaiah is talking to God. He says, "*Thy* dead shall live. My dead bodies shall rise [speaking as the national leader]. Awake and sing, ye that dwell in the dust [of the grave]; for the dew of God is a life-giving dew, and the earth shall cast forth the dead" (Isaiah 26:19).

He speaks of a resurrection of the dead bodies of those in touch with God. He recognizes that their spirits have been living. Now comes a reunion, a time of joyous singing.

Jesus' Teachings—a Test Case

One of the most positive teachings on the subject was given by Jesus in the running, fiery dispute with some of the national leaders during His last few weeks on earth (Mark 12:18–27, and parallels). It was His answer to the Sadducees' favorite question.

The Sadducees were the atheistic materialists of the Jewish nation. Disbelief in the resurrection was the outstanding feature in their creed. They made a carefully planned attack on Jesus. They felt so sure of cornering Him that they attacked in the open, in front of the thickening Passover crowds.

They had a test case to present. They considered it unanswerable. A man died, they said, leaving his widow childless. By Jewish custom, his brother married the widow to continue the family line. But the brother also died childless, and in turn seven brothers married the widow and died without leaving an heir. In the resurrection that Jesus taught, which brother would be her husband?

You can see the Sadducees chuckling, an unholy hatred and glee in their eyes. Now, they were quite sure, they had Him! And out in the open. It would be a public defeat for this Man they despised.

Jesus' reply was so simple, quiet, clear, and absolutely convincing that His questioners were utterly silenced. And that is saying a lot for a Sadducee.

He answered, in effect: "It's no wonder you make such blunders, for you evidently don't know your own Scriptures. And you don't know the power of God. For the other world has not the same limitations as this. There they neither marry nor are given in marriage, but are upon the level of the angels. For *neither can they die anymore.*"

He went on: "*As touching the dead, that they are*

raised; have ye not read in the book of Moses, in the place concerning the bush, how God spoke unto him saying, I am the God of Abraham, and the God of Isaac, and the God of Jacob?" He added with that convincing, unanswerable quietness: "He is not the God of the dead, but of the living."

God is a God of life. Abraham and the others were indeed dead, in the common language and experience of humans—but they were not really dead. They were living when the word was spoken to Moses out of the burning, unburned bush, more than four centuries after their death on earth.

They were living as Jesus spoke. They were living with God. They had the same quality of life as Him. Those whose hearts are in touch with God have the same qualities as God. *All* continue to have some part of creative life; these special ones have the same sort of full life as God Himself. He is a living God. They are living, too.

The impact of Jesus' answer is seen in His critics' attitude. They actually were silenced! Jesus' words were convincing and powerful. The Sadducees retired dumfounded, utterly routed. It was such a victory for Jesus that another group of His enemies mustered their forces to try to gain some of the lost ground.

God is a living God. Those who are in touch of

heart with Him are like Him. They take on His quality of life. Although they have died here, they are living with Him, living His kind of life. His power makes it possible, overcoming the power of death. The Book clearly teaches it, and Jesus teaches it here.

The Betrayal Night Talk

The betrayal night talk between Jesus and the inner circle (John 13–17) contains clear information. Jesus' intimate disciple John says plainly that Jesus knew the time had come for Him to leave this world and *go back up Home to the Father* (John 13:1).

After Judas left, Jesus talked about *His Father's House,* evidently in another world. He was going there soon. But He was thinking about His disciples and planning for them. He was going away on their behalf. He was going to prepare a place for them to come to.

Then He would return and take them up with Him. So they all would be together again in the

Father's House, gathered around the old Home fireside. Could there be a simpler, more realistic picture of life—the real life—after death? (See John 14:1–3.)

These things confused the disciples. Jesus explained He had arranged for the between time, before this plan took effect. He would send Someone else to come and stay with them. This coming One would be everything Jesus had been to them—and more, in earthly terms. It is striking that the Holy Spirit in us and with us is the clearest evidence about this whole question we are considering (John 14:16–26).

That quiet place in your heart, that hunger to be pure, that tug to pray, all tell of the Spirit's presence within you. They also tell us a loved one who has died is now in His presence, face-to-face, fully enjoying the real, griefless life up there.

Then came the great, simple talk with the Father under the full, mellow moon (John 17). More than anything else can, it clarifies the other world, the reality of the Father and of things up there.

The words Jesus spoke to *the poor thief* hanging by His side on Calvary (Luke 23:39–43) must have come as an amazing comfort to that man: *"Today, thou shalt be with me* in paradise." The word *paradise* clearly stands for some desirable, blissful place. Jesus Himself was going there.

He would go there *at once*. The thief would be *with Him*. They would live together in this wonderful place. This man would be with Jesus *because of his attitude* toward Jesus, his being in heartfelt touch with Him.

That attitude recognized Jesus as Lord. The thief accepted Him as Master—a radical change from his early life. It was a repentant change. The prayerful mood was in control now, and Jesus' affirmation of him was positive: ". . .thou *shalt*. . ."

The love chapter of 1 Corinthians contrasts our understanding of the present and the future. In 1 Corinthians 13:8–12 we read:

> *There is a time coming when prophecy shall be done away, for it will all have been fulfilled; speaking in various tongues shall cease, for there will be one tongue common to all; and the painful acquiring of knowledge shall be a thing past because we shall know fully, and learn easily.*
>
> *At present we see as something is reflected in a piece of polished steel, or in a mirror, indistinctly, as though through a cloud. But*

*then face to face, that is my face, your face,
to Jesus' face [Cf. Exodus 33:11]. Now we
know only in part; but then we shall know
fully even as now we are fully known. When
that which is perfect is come that which is
in part shall be done away, or swallowed
up, the less in the greater, the thin line of
light in the noon shining.*

Jesus' Resurrection—Incidentals

Paul's great resurrection climax in the letter to his
Corinthian converts and friends is one of the choice
parts of this sacred Book. It is one of the most
fascinating stories told by Paul.

Jesus' resurrection is the cornerstone of all Christian truth. But we are not concerned with that at
the moment. Rather, we are concerned with the incidentals—the tremendous incidentals—that come
with the resurrection.

There is another world, a spirit world. Jesus is
alive up there, in command. Everything in Heaven
and on earth is at His disposal. His power is more

than we can understand. But He is the same Jesus who fed, healed, taught, *and* died on earth.

The upper spirit world dwarfs this old earth. The spirit world is the center of everything. All things on earth are regulated there, including the desperate fight against the revolutionary powers of evil. It is the real world.

Jesus' whole heart and thought are in things down here. Everyone who follows Him simply and fully, who is in touch of heart with Him, is unspeakably precious to Him. His plans of action are centered on earth. Now is a waiting time. Infinitely patient, He is letting the great, sore problem of evil work itself out on earth.

But one day He will intervene. Intervention is plainly part of the schedule. Studiously, carefully watching everyone involved, both humans and spirits, He is delaying intervention, for He is just to everyone—even to the great, evil spirit prince.

The program of earthly action on the intervention day is outlined broadly in 1 Corinthians 15:22–27. All of His who have died will rise from their graves, just as He did. As He comes down toward earth, His spiritual magnetism will draw their bodies up to reunite with their glad spirits.

Then will come the new order of things on earth —His order of things. When His purpose is achieved, when all opponents are abolished totally, then He will turn the kingdom over to the Father. The climax of the kingdom is this: Death, our last enemy, is put to death.

There is also what we may call *the personal program* He has arranged for His trusting ones (1 Corinthians 15:50–57). The intervention day will be heralded by a trumpet summoning the saints to form in rank. Quicker than the blink of an eye, the bodies lying in the graves of those in touch will have a new life as their spirits, now in Christ's presence, reenter their old bodies. They will rise up toward this spiritual center of gravity, the glorified Jesus.

And all who then are living on earth, who have that same vital heart-touch, instantly will experience some bodily change, answering the pull of the upward gravity. Courteously, they will wait until those who have died precede them. Then together they will be in Jesus' presence, the living joining their dead loved ones.

Christ is called, in regard to His resurrection, "the firstfruits" (1 Corinthians 15:20–23). His is the model on which His followers' resurrections will be shaped. He rose; they will rise. His body was changed, given new powers, its limitations gone; it will be the same with their bodies. His identity remained, and He was recognized; so it will be with them.

The empty tomb is a guarantee of countless other empty graves. Jesus' living up there guarantees that others are living. They share the same sort of life as He, a victorious, overflowing life. He is the "firstfruits."

From Paul's Writings

There is no more eloquent reference to the change from this world to the next than Paul's letter in 2 Corinthians (2 Corinthians 5:1–8). He thought of the body as a tent, easily taken down and moved. Death is the taking down of the tent. To Paul, Christ's second coming meant a new sort of life for him, absorbing the bodily life here.

Paul compared the body to clothing. Dying is like putting off the old suit of clothes, anticipating something better. There is a new suit to wear, a new life immediately following death. If Christ had come while Paul still lived, then the new suit would have been put on *over* the old. The new life would swallow the present life without the break of death.

Paul intensely wanted the great change to come not by death, but by Christ's return. But whichever way it happened would lead to the same happy result. Paul instantly would be in Christ's immediate presence, reveling in the wondrous new life. To be here, in this body, meant absence from the immediate presence of his Lord. For his spirit to leave his body meant an instant transition into the immediate, conscious presence of the Lord he adored so much.

In the letter Paul circulated to the churches centered in Ephesus, he pictured the Christ of Gethsemane and Calvary *now seated* in the upper world at the Father's right hand, possessing all power both in the spirit world and on earth (Ephesians 1:20–22).

A similar picture is found in Colossians 1:14–18. The broad view in this double picture is refreshing. In Ephesians Paul pictured Christ *after* His errand to the earth. In Colossians we see Him *before* the earthly mission. His presence on earth is like a tremendous, tragic, glorious hyphen in His career. It was God who did things in that long-ago week of creation. Then came His errand to earth. Then He returned, and sits quietly until the next part of the program completes of His plan.

A passage in 1 Thessalonians is of peculiar interest. Paul was writing to comfort readers sorrowing over the death of loved ones (1 Thessalonians 4:13–18). The teaching was tied to the expected second coming of Christ. As surely as Jesus died and rose again, Paul said, God through Jesus will bring up from the grave into His presence, *with* Jesus, those trusting ones who have died.

Paul described how it will be done. The Lord will descend from the upper spirit world, where He is now. First, those dead who trusted Him will rise from their graves; then the living who trust will be caught up. They will be together. Apart from second-coming teaching, it is a very real, joyous picture of life after death.

The writer of Hebrews, probably a close friend and disciple of Paul, told what happened on the other side of the cloud that Luke said carried Jesus up through the blue. Jesus "*sat down* [as one whose task for the present was done] on the right hand [the place of power] of the Majesty on high" (Hebrews 1:3). Plainly, something very real is on the other side of the upper blue. There also is Someone very real, and others who are very really with Him.

Peter also left some interesting teaching about the question we are considering. Speaking of Jesus in 1 Peter 3:18, he said, "Being put to death in the flesh, *but* made alive in the spirit."

That "but" throbs with eager life. It is a hinge opening the door into the beyond. Peter was referring to what happened to Jesus at the moment of His death on the cross. As he experienced death in His body, He experienced just the reverse in His spiritual life.

The two parts of this sentence stand in contrast. The language implies that as life in the body *decreased* to the point of extinction, life in the spirit *increased*. Not only did Jesus' spirit continue to live; there was an increase of life, either more life or a different, higher sort of life—or both.

In 1 John 3:2, we are told we do not know at present just what will be in the future life, but we do know that when Christ appears openly to humankind, those in touch will be like *Him,* for *we shall see* Him even as He is.

The Patmos Book

John's Patmos book begins with a wonderful look at the glorified Jesus, then gives four looks into the upper spirit world. In that look at Jesus Himself, glorified, John was overwhelmed by His Person. But when Jesus began to talk, it was the same sort of talk John was used to from his Master. The gentle right hand touched him again, and the quieting words came: "*Fear not:* I am the first and the last, *and the Living One;* and I *became dead* and behold! *I am alive;* I am alive *endlessly;* and more than that, I have the keys, *the absolute control, of death and of the whole spirit world, where men go at death*" (Revelation 1:17, 18). That's unmistakable, plain talk about life after death from the One we are inclined to trust fully.

Then come the four looks at those whose hearts are allied to Jesus. In the first (Revelation 6:9–11), Christian martyrs are seen in His immediate presence, honored and comforted and told to be patient a bit longer as things on earth reach the great climax.

In the second look (Revelation 7:9–17), we see countless ones who have been rescued from the Great Tribulation. They have been purified by Jesus' blood. Now they are in the presence of the glorified Jesus, singing rapturously, with shining, victorious faces, full of life. They are busy performing errands and tasks and are on intimate terms with Jesus Himself.

The third passage (Revelation 14:1–5) gives a similar description. All of the redeemed are in the presence of the Lord Jesus, singing the great songs of salvation and in full fellowship with their Lord, whom they obey absolutely, without question.

The last example looks up into the real world, the headquarters. We all love this closing section of John's Revelation. John's own spirit was so stirred by the picture that his grammar faltered. His native Hebrew spirit and thought had a hard time trying to tell the full story in Greek, the language spoken by most of the church to whom he wrote. He actually made new grammatical adjustments. (When we see Jesus' face, there will be a good many adjustments —some of them pretty radical.)

Here, we see people on earth gathered around the Father as a large family gathers around the fireplace after a long day (Revelation 21:3–7). God and humans are living together. Death is gone. Tears and pain are just memories! There is the sweetest intimacy between God and humans, as between a father and his dear children.

Then the scene shifts to the garden (Revelation 22:1–5). Again, they are all together in wonderful fellowship. Humans are face-to-face with their wonderful Saviour God. They are busy doing His work. The curses of sin and sickness are gone. There is one long, happy daytime in the sunshine of Jesus' presence.

Underscoring the Facts

This Book of God describes *certain outstanding events* that illustrate this teaching. Illustration is the very lifeblood of teaching.

For one man actually to leave the earth in front of witnesses is worth a hundred statements that this act can be done. For one man actually to die and be buried, then to rise from the grave and touch and talk with witnesses is simply unanswerable.

When teaching is backed by an event of that sort, every doubting, critical voice is silenced. The teaching stands on the strength of the event. The event itself is explained fully and clearly by the teaching. The teaching and the event are interlaced unbreakably. The case could not be stronger.

This solitary Book contains *twelve separate occurrences,* fully vouched for, that illustrate our study. Five of these are in the Old Testament, seven in the New.

In the Old, two men went up into the spirit world without dying: Enoch and Elijah. Two other persons died and were brought back to life, one through the prayer and faith of Elijah, the other through Elisha. There is the obscure instance of an unknown man brought back to life through Elisha's touch.

In the New Testament, three persons were brought back to life through Jesus' power: Jairus's daughter, the son of the widow of Nain, and Lazarus. Dorcas of Joppa on the Mediterranean coast was brought back through Peter's action, and the young man Eutychus of Troas on the Dardanelles coast was restored through Paul's intervention.

There is the appearance of Moses and Elijah on the Mount of Transfiguration. And at the climax is the resurrection of Jesus Himself and His ascension —a twin event. Let us look at these briefly to distinguish the essential facts.

It is recorded as a fact that Enoch went up from the earth into God's immediate presence (Cf. Genesis 5:21–24, with Hebrews 11:5). He did not die. His body was not buried. He went up bodily through the blue, into Heaven. That simple, tremendous thing is put on record.

Enoch was not an obscure person. He was the best-known man of his day. He was the head of the first family of his time, head of his race. His out-standing characteristic was that he "walked with God." This is connected directly with the unusual manner of his leaving the earth. God and he were on the friendliest terms. It was the truest sort of heartfelt friendship.

One can imagine what a sensation his ascension made. Try to envision what effect such an event would have had *at the time*.

It may have happened one day as he stood with a group on a village street, perhaps talking to skeptics about the reality and presence of God. While they talked, they may have been astounded to see his face turn upward, perhaps responding to something they could not see, his face radiant as if he were looking into the face of his dearest Friend. A hush would have fallen over them as his feet left the ground and he rose into the air, unsupported by anything they could see. He would have moved up and up until he was seen no more. And these critics would have realized in their innermost spirits what had happened—God had taken their kinsman up to live with Him in the spirit world.

It was a fact that a man whom everybody knew had disappeared through the upper blue and never returned. Furthermore, the strange happening fit perfectly with this man's desire. It seemed natural. As he had walked with God during his common life, it seemed fitting that he actually should go up and walk with Him in the real world, the spirit world.

This fact is vouched for by the Book of God. One fact vouches for another. It was the talk of the entire race. It was not done in secret. It was a tremendous witness and undoubtedly made a profound impression on everyone. God was brought into life in a strange, very real, new way.

God seems to have had a purpose for this. Enoch was God's special *witness* to the whole race, God's loving, faithful witness at a time when it was not easy. He told what he *knew* about the real God and His friendship (Jude 14, 15).

The Heavenly Chariots

More than twenty centuries after Enoch came another man uncommonly in touch with God—Elijah. He went up bodily through the blue vault as Elisha watched. This fact is attested in the Book of God (2 Kings 2:1–12) by a most reliable witness. It is described in detail. It is certainly dramatic. In a whirlwind, flaming chariots swept down from above and carried him out of sight.

Elijah is one of the chief characters in God's Book, a great, righteous leader. He severely denounced the evil Ahab in his palace. He locked up the windows of Heaven for forty-two months, then dramatically unlocked them. The last Hebrew prophet, Malachi, said he would return for a further bit of outstanding witnessing. This so captivated the Hebrew people that they freely discussed whether Jesus was Elijah returning, as foretold.

John the Herald is said by Jesus to have fulfilled the ministry spoken of by Elijah. There is good reason to think that like Enoch, Elijah's earthly task is not finished. Each man, in his time, was the main witness to God and God's truth—when belief in both was especially weak. The exceptional way these two men left the earth likely points to their future service down here in some great moral emergency. Their ascension was not just a reward, though it may have been partly that. Apparently, they still will know death.

For now, note that this dependable Book states as a fact that they went up bodily into the spirit world. So there *is* such a world. Their bodies must have undergone some radical change to enter this new, completely different sphere.

As we will see later, Elijah clearly retained his identity and his level of intelligence in that spiritual realm. And what would be true of Elijah likely would be true of Enoch.

There are three instances of the dead being restored to life by Jesus. They are well-authenticated facts, highly significant to our study. The three were at different stages of death. Jairus's daughter had just died (Luke 8:41–42, 49–56, and parallels). The son of the widow of Nain was being carried to his burial (Luke 7:11–17). Lazarus had lain in the grave four days (John 11:17–44).

The fact of death was established clearly in each instance. There could be no question in the cases of Lazarus or the young man of Nain. And when Jesus said to the people in Jairus's house the girl was not dead, but asleep, they laughed at him, *"knowing that she was dead."*

All the usual evidence of death in each case was so plain it was not questioned. Their spirits were brought back to the bodies they had left, and the bodies were retouched with vigor to serve as dwelling places for their spirits. Their spirits still lived while their bodies lay dead; the spirits were recalled from where they were.

So there was not only continuation of the spirit life but unity of the human spirit and its body. Each spirit and body belong together. Indeed, we know the body takes on the character of the human spirit living in it; this is especially easy to read in the human face, but the imprint of the spirit is in the whole body.

It was not some other human spirit that came back to Lazarus's body. Lazarus's returning spirit did not enter some other body in the graveyard. There was a clear identification of spirit and body. When they shared that glad reunion supper in Bethany, with Jesus as the Guest of honor, no one doubted the identity of Lazarus.

The Transfiguration

We now turn to the story of Jesus' transfiguration. We are not concerned at the moment with its significance; we simply note certain incidental facts.

It is stated as a fact that Moses and Elijah were there. Moses had died some fifteen hundred years before. Elijah had not died but had disappeared from human view, through the upper blue, some eight hundred years before. Now both men were seen plainly. It was clear they had been living all that time, but not on earth.

Their identity was clear. The three disciples recognized them at once. (Of course, Moses and Elijah also recognized each other.) Moses and Elijah fully understood Jesus' purposes and plans. They knew what was going to happen to Him at Jerusalem.

There was no distress or grief. They were themselves. Their minds were the same as in their early lives. They fully grasped the great events being worked out by Jesus' errand to earth. Their understanding encompassed events on earth as they were connected with the upper world, and events of the future. They fully realized the great purpose of Christ in going to Calvary, although nobody on earth seemed to understand. They saw things on earth *from God's point of view,* and they knew His plans would triumph. They talked of the death Jesus would "*accomplish.*"

When the conversation was over, they disappeared as they had come. Where did they go? Presumably back up where they had been. Where can we infer they are now? Clearly, still living, in full possession of their faculties, in that spirit world where Christ joined them at His ascension.

It would seem from Malachi 4:5 and 6 that Elijah has a bit of work to do on earth before things get straightened out. It will be the same sort of thing he did so boldly in Ahab's wicked day. Elijah seems reserved for that sort of work.

These two men evidently are more now than when they were on earth. They have a broader grasp, keener perception, and clearer knowledge of the way things will work out. Elijah now has no use for that juniper tree. He has "graduated."

The instances of Dorcas (Acts 9:36–43) and the young man at Troas (Acts 20:7–12) give us the same essential facts. They add tremendous *emphasis* to the other events. This is indeed living, irrefutable testimony.

Jesus' resurrection stands wholly by itself. The fact of His death is inarguable. It is basically a medical question, and the simple use of exact language gives the doctor the essential information. The spear thrust into His side brought out not just blood, but "blood and water." The separation in the fluid had taken place. That at once tells that death had occurred.

I do not intend to gather here the detailed evidence of Jesus' resurrection. There is no point repeating it. Excellent summaries can be found in any good library or minister's study. Suffice it to say for now that no fact in common history is authenticated better by reliable evidence than the resurrection of Jesus. The plain evidence is complete and undeniable. The same can be said for the appearances of Jesus after the resurrection, and for His ascension.

This could be called the fact of greatest significance. It means Jesus' spirit was living while His body lay in the grave. Then His spirit reentered His body. He moved among humans again. He was *recognized*. His *identity* was clear. He was *more* at that point than before. All limitations were gone. A new power lifted Him far above ordinary conditions.

He went up bodily, in plain sight of humans, through the doorway of the blue above. *He is alive.* He is somewhere *up*. Someday He is coming back the way He went, He *said*. What already has happened to Him makes a good argument that He will do as He said, for He is more now than before.

The Damascus Road Event

One other event in this unique Book of God asks for space here: the experience of Saul on the Damascus Road. It may be considered a climax to

Jesus' resurrection, for it resulted directly from the resurrection. And it was a dynamic result.

Saul was a cultured, disciplined man. In modern terms, he was university-bred, of an old, honored family, a leader among the younger set in Jerusalem. He was in close touch with the Jerusalem leaders who planned Jesus' death.

He came to the attention of history shortly after Jesus died, as a persecutor of Jesus' followers. He became an aggressive leader of the persecutors, recognized and authorized by the national leaders. He hated Jesus, His teachings, and His followers to an extreme degree. His spirit at this point is described vividly in the record: "Saul, yet breathing threatenings and slaughter against the disciples of the Lord."

The occurrence on the Damascus Road (Acts 9:1–22, with parallels) came suddenly. It became the outstanding experience of Saul's life. He never got over it. A light, coming from above, suddenly blazed in front of him. It was not sunlight; it was brighter, he later said.

With the strange light came a power that forced him to fall to the earth. There was a clear, distinct voice, followed by a brief conversation between Saul and Someone connected with the light and the voice. This One said plainly, "I am Jesus whom thou persecutest."

From that hour, Saul was transformed completely. Once a bitter enemy using all his powers against Jesus, he became His most devoted follower and exponent. No similar transformation of such a strong man is recorded. Saul's case stands alone.

And observe that there is no stronger, clearer, more convincing evidence than that of the conversion of Saul on the Damascus Road, when we consider his wide influence on the spread of Christianity.

Note the teaching involved. The Man Jesus, Who had been killed, was now alive, somewhere in an upper spirit world. He was in full possession of His faculties. He had superhuman, divine power. Saul —this exceptional, rarely trained, Herculean-willed persecutor—recognized unmistakably Jesus' identity, His concern with earthly affairs, His intimacy with His followers, His overwhelming works. And Saul now completely reversed his course and became His devoted follower.

Never was a strong career so radically reversed. Saul's devotion became as marked as his hatred had been. Nothing could dim his burning devotion to Jesus. The breaking of family ties and friendships, the certain loss of inheritance, the bitter social ostracism, the intense persecution, years of the most extreme personal hardship and, at the end, a violent death—all of this simply fueled the flame of his devotion to the Man of light and power.

These are the teachings and events that sweetly assure us about our dead loved ones who are in touch with God.

In Touch of Heart

But who are these people whom we know to be happy in the spirit world? *All* who have gone? Painfully, the answer is an emphatic no.

They are those who are *in touch of heart with God*. I have not used that good Bible word *believe*. The phrases "in touch of heart with God" and "believing on the Lord Jesus" mean the same thing. But *believe* has been twisted from its simple, fine, true meaning. It has come to mean a belief in *things,* creeds, church formulas, etc. It really refers to being *in touch of heart with God,* and that touch can come only through Jesus Christ.

We are talking about a changed attitude toward God where the life has been wrong. It means everything that belief, trust, love, and devotion can mean. There must be a *real personal touch of heart* with our Father-God, who is known only through Jesus Christ, the Man who died on Calvary.

I have not spoken of church membership, which is another of the fine things that has suffered at human hands. There are church members whose hearts are not in touch with the heart of Jesus. At the same time, many nonmembers of a church, many who have no opportunity for that privilege, are in real touch of heart with God.

When did they come into that saving touch? With some it may have been a lifelong experience, with others a much shorter story. Some come creeping in at the close of life, as a tired child creeps into the mother's lap and snuggles contentedly. The mother would not turn away her child. Certainly the Man who died will not turn away any who, in their hearts, turn to Him.

Thoughtful, intelligent distinctions will be made up there, as we have seen. But anyone who comes for that touch of heart, however poorly expressed, will be in the blessed presence of Christ at the close of earthly life. And where believing prayer has been sent up for loved ones, there *will* be that touch *sometime*. There is *no question* of that.

The Reason: Jesus' Blood

I have given these last questions the most prominent place at the close of the section: *Why* are these
people in the glad presence of Christ and of their
loved ones in the upper Homeland? *How* do they
get there?

The answer is simple, but it goes to the very
taproot of Christian teaching. *It is because Jesus
died and rose again.* It is that, to the exclusion of
everything else.

These people cannot diminish their sin or insist
on their way in defiance of God's way. Sin cannot
be ignored by human law or by God. Personal
rebellion and defiance of God—the core of sin—
cannot be winked at.

We will *not* enter into Christ's presence because
we have been consistent church members. It will
not be because of some great personal sacrifice we
have made or because we have stopped an enemy
bullet with our bodies. It will *not* even be because
we have believed in the Lord Jesus Christ.

It will be *only* because Jesus took on Himself the
price we should pay for our sins. His blood poured

till no red drops remained. His life burned out sacrificially till no white ashes remained. This alone is the reason why these people go up into His Presence.

The other things are good. Believing is the connecting link with the thing that does the saving. There must be this connecting link, this touch of heart. But the one thing that *saves* is the precious lifeblood of Jesus at His death. Then His rising again tied the knot for us, completing His victory over sin and death, and over the prince of death.

A young Italian girl sat at her fruit stand, absorbed in a small Book. A man paused to get some fruit and asked what she was reading so intently. She replied timidly, "The Word of God, sir."

He was a skeptic who delighted in spreading his skeptical poison. He asked, "Who told you the Bible is the Word of God?"

With childlike simplicity, she replied, "God told me Himself."

"God told you! Impossible! How did He tell you? You have never seen Him or talked with Him. How could He tell you?"

For a few moments the girl was confused and silent. Then looking up, she said respectfully, "Sir, who told you there is a sun in the sky?"

The man replied contemptuously, "Who told

me? Nobody. I do not need to be told. The sun tells this about itself. It warms me. I love its light."

And the young Italian girl said earnestly, "You have put it straight, sir—for the sun and for the Bible. That's the way God tells me this in His Book. I read it. It warms my heart. It gives me light. I love its light and warmth. None but God could give me the light and warmth I get from this Book."

He turned away, embarrassed by her simple faith.

It did not matter which church she belonged to. There was *the touch of heart with God*. That is the thing that counts, now and up yonder.

Chapter 3

What Can We Know About Others Who Have Died?

A Painful Story

Others who have died are not in touch of heart with Jesus. This is distressing but true.

Why are there others? It is not because of anything God does. It is because of something humans do, and because of something they do not do in response to God's call. It was never intended that there should be others. It is a break in the original plan. Men and women have the power to break God's plans, so far as they are concerned. God gave them freedom to choose and act.

Notice two fundamental points in the original plan. First, humans should be like God in freedom of choice and action. Second, God and humans always should be in full touch with each other.

Clearly, the second hinges on the first. The full touch can occur only if the human chooses to have it. God will not take away that freedom to act, even if it breaks His heart.

This is a painful story. I will try to point out the bad swings in the pendulum, both ways, and then point out the truth lying between. It must be told honestly, but tenderly. It will be distressing.

The common teaching of the church from, say, the fourth century up to the Protestant revolt was definite and intense. Loyal church membership was taught as being essential to salvation. There was no awed hush in pronouncing the word Hell, no mincing of words in picturing its fiery terrors. The vast numbers who never had heard of the church or of Christ were not taken into consideration.

The Protestant Movement taught the same thing, with one outstanding exception. The emphasis changed from church membership to faith in Christ as the saving factor. But much of the harshness of common church teaching continued throughout the Protestant Movement, and even hardened. A common reference has been made to a certain well-known French-Swiss leader of the Protestant Movement depicting infants burning in the flames of the lost world.

Ian Maclaren, in one of his stories of Scotland, pictured a small lad listening at the evening service of a country church. The little church was lit with candles. A candle sputtered on the pulpit. Eternal punishment was the subject of discussion. All the boy remembered was the tall, lean, stern-faced preacher silently holding a piece of paper in the candle's flame until it was consumed, then describing in awful tones what happened to the unrepentant. Terrified, the boy shrank tighter into the corner of the hard-seated pew, trying to escape the God in this picture.

Hopefully, that is an extreme illustration of church teaching. But it points to a general trend.

Bad Pendulum Swings

The *decided swing away* from such teaching was natural. The human heart revolted. And typically, when the pendulum of teaching starts the other way, it goes to the extreme. The swing away in this case took three forms.

Universalism taught that all humans ultimately would be saved. There would be no "others." There would be a corrective retribution for wrong. When the correction was complete, the human would be saved. Combining portions of Scripture with suitable logic, a strong case is made for those who want to think that way.

The problem with this teaching is that it uses those statements of Scripture which suit its purpose and *ignores* the rest. Anything can be "proved" from the Bible by that method.

Another popular theory is called *constitutional immortality*. It teaches that only those in touch with

Christ have eternal life; others simply cease to exist. *Annihilationism* is another term for the same general teaching, which is built on a skillful play of Biblical language. The plain, common meanings of certain words are ignored, or the words are restricted to the preferred meanings. Much is made of certain Greek words used in the same restricted way as English words.

The problem with this teaching is that it is unphilosophical, illogical, and unbiblical. It is unphilosophical because a *spirit* cannot cease to exist; it is the essence of God. It is illogical because it twists the plain, accepted meaning of common language. It is unbiblical because it ignores certain parts of Scripture unsuited to its purpose.

A third concept has been accepted widely: *final restorationism.* It teaches that at some time in the far future, after certain discipline has been carried out, all humans, angels, and even Satan himself will be restored completely. All will be in perfect touch with God. Like the other two, this teaching is based on certain passages of Scripture, a skillful playing with the meaning of certain words, the attractive use of logic, and a careful ignoring of other parts of Scripture.

A more common idea this century has been what might be called the *continuance* teaching. There is said to be no real difference in morals or character as one crosses the line of death. Death itself makes a certain radical difference, of course, but apart from that, there is said to be no difference. The untold millions who have died are pictured wandering about the earth, disembodied, floating through space. They continue the old habits of this life, smoking, drinking, using vulgar language. There is no marked moral change, no suffering connected to their former life, no new attitude toward Christ, goodness or sin.

Note carefully that the first and third teachings are very attractive. A very plausible case can be made for each. They have tremendous emotional appeal. You earnestly might wish they were true.

May I say very reverently that I believe God devoutly wishes they might be true. Anything else is a break in His plans. But they fail to consider two things: our freedom of choice and the real nature of sin.

We all laugh at the ostrich for hiding its small head in the sand so it won't see danger. To ignore *any facts,* and to ignore the plain teaching of God's Word, is as foolish as the small-brained ostrich. Just *one fact* ignored completely changes the conclusion, no matter how skillfully and logically reached. It makes it worthless and, worse, dangerous because it is misleading.

The popularity of these and similar teachings has resulted in a wide swing away from the old Protestant and Catholic teaching. Certain so-called liberal denominations boast that although they may not have increased in *numbers,* their teachings have permeated the other denominations. All indications tend to confirm this.

Wartime Teachings

A common feeling in many of our churches today is that any person will "pull through safely somehow." Regardless of his or her belief or lack of it, regardless of lifestyle, the individual finally will get safely past punishment or Hell. Things will be "all right."

Earlier this century a certain type of evangelist preached throughout America. These evangelists were endorsed for preaching "the old Gospel." Their frequent reference to future punishment was one of their prominent features. But the use of words like *Hell* and *damned* was so akin to common profanity that it was blasphemous. And the typical listener mocked the subject. People thought it was funny, so far had the pendulum swung.

The World War greatly increased some good tendencies and many very bad ones. In both England and America, it commonly was taught and accepted that if a soldier had made his supreme sacrifice in action, his salvation was absolutely secured.

Certainly, no one would want to diminish the splendid sacrifice made by thousands of soldiers during the war. But it was a great wrong to deceive these men on the very edge of possible death by not saying more.

A minister friend of mine was visiting a large army camp. He was trying to tell the real Gospel story tactfully, convincingly, and fully.

A solemn soldier came to his quarters one night after a service. He said, "We men have been discussing this thing, and we had it settled that if we die in action, our salvation is secured. That is what we have been told. Now, you say there must be something else to fix things for us. We men are all mixed up." My friend tried, in his brotherly way, to make it clear.

At an international convention of rescue mission workers, the delegates agreed this idea was so firmly believed by ex-servicemen that it greatly hindered efforts to win them to a simple faith in Christ.

This is a common belief regarding punishment for wrongdoing in the afterlife. It simply is not so. It represents the extreme swing of the pendulum from the earlier extreme church teaching. At one extreme, Hell is practically the biggest thing in the universe, with Heaven a comparatively small affair. At the other extreme, there is no Hell at all.

You say, "That is putting it too strongly, isn't it? Hell—the biggest thing?"

No, that was the direct, logical conclusion for centuries. Members of the Christian church have been a distinct minority of the whole race, even if we reckon—as people once did—that all subjects of Catholic countries were and are members of the church. It would be a *small* minority indeed, considering the *gradual* spread of the church through Europe during the early centuries.

All those who have *heard* of Jesus Christ in any way since He was on earth likewise would be a minority. All who have accepted Him, even nominally, would be a much smaller minority.

Now think of the whole earth, and think through the long centuries. Clearly, the vast majority of humans must be considered outside, doomed to endless woe. That is the logical conclusion. Is it surprising that the swing was so strong toward the "no Hell" extreme?

We will find the truth between these two extremes.

Spirit Level Accuracy

Let's turn again to this Book of God. We want to get *all* of what it says and fit it together in one simple, clear story. This is the only sane thing to do: Consider *all* the Book says, take its statements at their plain, common meaning and let that tell the story, *regardless* of what it may do to our theories.

Have you ever watched a skillful bricklayer at work? He uses a delicate instrument called a *spirit level* that indicates whether a surface is perfectly level. As the mason lays his bricks, layer by layer, he constantly holds the spirit level to the surface to test its straightness. He puts it on top of the bricks, in front, up and down. He knows it is the only safe thing to do. All surveyors and builders use a similar device for determining levels accurately. They must. Otherwise, they and their work would be rejected.

Recently, I watched a scrub bricklayer work on the foundation of a small frame house that had been moved. He had no spirit level. He measured "by his eye." That seemed satisfactory to him, but the work he did was anything but satisfactory. It was painfully out of level, although in this case it apparently was not dangerous.

As I watched him, I thought of other builders, builders of character, who judge "by the eye," which they *think* is a sufficient standard. They do pretty wobbly work in character building. The problem is that their inefficient, nonstandard work endangers the lives they work with.

Happily, there is a spirit level by which to test all human teachers and teachings. Whatever work is not done by the standard spirit level is worthless and may prove very dangerous to human life. This is a three-part spirit level: the *Holy Spirit,* in the *Book,* in the hands of *a person strongly yielded* to the Spirit's sway. The Spirit Himself is the standard. He speaks in this Book, which thus becomes the standard. Its teachings can be fully, clearly grasped only by someone in touch with that Spirit, although anyone may read and get the general drift of the teaching.

We want to find out just what the complete

teaching of the Book is regarding this most vital subject. This study and the final one of the series, "Is There Another Chance for Salvation After Death?" touch two phases of the issue. They are separated in order to provide a clearer look at each phase and, in turn, to grasp the whole thing more clearly. The current study gathers the *facts* in the case. The last touches the *principle* and *process* underlying the facts.

Truth Cuts Cleanly

The first thing one notes in the Book is the sharp distinction between those not in heartfelt touch with God, commonly called "the wicked," and those whose hearts are in touch with Him, commonly called "the righteous." In these studies, the two alternate phrases are taken as exact equivalents. The sharp distinction is especially marked in the Psalms and Gospels, but it runs from cover to cover.

Another thing that stands out sharply is that the distinction plainly extends beyond the line of death. The moral differences of this life persist beyond the grave.

These are our two most striking things to note at the outset: The spirit level marks an immediate difference and a persistent difference.

Now, notice the language used in the Old Testament for the place where the wicked dead are said to go. For instance, in Psalm 9:16 and 17: "Jehovah hath executed judgment; the wicked is snared in the work of his own hands. The wicked shall be turned into hell, even all the peoples that forget God."

The Hebrew word for Hell here is *Sheol,* as translated in the revised versions. *Sheol* means, literally, the underworld, a cavity or a hollow subterranean place. It has two distinct meanings, one neutral and one positive.

In its neutral meaning, it refers simply to the world of departed human beings, regardless of their condition. In its positive meaning, it is the place of punishment. The wicked are said to have gone to "Sheol." They are *not* in God's presence but are said to be in torment.

Those who have died and whose hearts are in touch with God are said to be in Sheol (the world of departed spirits), and they are said to be in the *immediate presence of God.* This word *Sheol,* neutral in itself, gets its positive meaning from some *added* words.

For instance, "a fire is kindled in my anger, and burneth unto the lowest hell (Sheol)" (Deuteronomy 32:22; see connection). Here it is associated directly with fire, with the punishment of evil. It warns of the adulterous woman and her victims: "Her steps take hold of hell" (Sheol); "her house is the way to hell" (Sheol); "her guests are in the depths of hell" (Sheol) (Proverbs 5:5, 7:27, 9:18). It speaks of the archenemy of God and of all good: "Hell [Sheol] from beneath is moved for thee to meet thee at thy coming. . . . Thou shalt be brought down to hell" (Sheol) (Isaiah 14:9, 15).

In about half its occurrences, the word is translated "the grave" in the Authorized Version. Otherwise, it usually is translated "hell," a few times "the pit."

In the New Testament, two Greek words commonly are translated "hell." They are *Hades* and *Gehenna*.

Hades is neutral. It means the world of departed spirits, where all go when they die. *Gehenna* originally was the name of the valley outside Jerusalem where little children once were thrown into a fire in idolatrous worship. When this horrible practice was abolished, the place was used to dump refuse, including dead animals and the unburied bodies of criminals. Its fires burned continually, intensely.

Christ clearly used this word as a name for the

place of punishment of the wicked. For instance, Jesus said certain people "shall be in danger of the hell (Gehenna) of fire." (See Matthew 5:22, 29 and 30. Also, for usage of *Gehenna,* see Matthew 10:28, 18:9, 23:15, and 33.) Plainly, in this case it cannot mean the Gehenna burning outside Jerusalem's walls. It must mean something else, a place for certain people corresponding to this fire for the refuse.

Toward the close, in the Revelation, other words are used in the same sense as the earlier use of *Gehenna:* "abyss," "the lake of fire," and "the second death." The last two are said to be the same thing. To this place, it is said, will go Satan, his human leaders in the last great warfare against God, and all people whose hearts are not in touch with God. (See Revelation 19:20 and 20:1–3, 6, 10, 14, and 15.) There is the distinct indication that this is the final disposition for these outcasts.

Jesus' Plain Teachings

Now turn to *Jesus' own teachings*. Let's remind ourselves of the outstanding characteristics of Jesus:

His humanness, His sympathy with suffering, His tender heart and speech, His unselfishness in relieving pain. This makes certain teachings stand out.

Look at some of His words: "Enter ye in by the narrow gate: for wide is the gate, and broad is the way, *that leadeth to destruction*. . . . For narrow is the gate, and straitened the way, that leadeth unto life" (Matthew 7:13, 14). Here, "destruction" is contrasted with "life." There are two paths and two radically different ends.

"Many will say to me in that day, Lord, Lord, did we not prophesy in thy name. . . ? And then will I profess to them, I never knew you; *depart from me,* ye that *work iniquity*" (Matthew 7:22, 23). Here, the absence of the heart touch is hidden under religious pretensions. The result is absence from Christ's presence in the future life.

Stronger language is used later, when those not in touch are "cast forth *into the outer darkness;* there shall be the weeping and gnashing of teeth" (Matthew 8:12). Unmistakable! The same dreaded language is used twice more in the form of parables (Matthew 22:13, 25:30) to describe those found lacking in the final settlement.

The fact of a settlement day for all, with perfect fairness in weighing actions and circumstances, and an awful result for some, is taught clearly: "It shall be more tolerable for the land of Sodom and Gomorrah [who were punished so terribly] in the day of judgment, than for you" (Matthew 10:15, 11:22 and 24, with variations).

Listen again. At the end of the present age, "the Son of man shall. . .gather out. . .all things that cause stumbling, and them that do iniquity, and shall cast them into *the furnace of fire:* There shall be the weeping and the gnashing of teeth" (Matthew 13:41 and 42, repeated with variations in verses 49 and 50). Could words be more plain or heartbreaking?

Jesus said three times it is better to be true and suffer some in this life than to suffer immeasurably more in the next life. "It is better for thee to enter into life maimed rather than. . .to go into the Gehenna, into the unquenchable fire." He added, in terribly graphic rhetoric, "where their worm dieth not, and the fire is not quenched" (Mark 9:43–49).

At the close of His talk on Mount Olivet, He pictured the adjustments of the final settlement in chilling terms: "Then shall the king [pictured in Verse 31 as Himself] say unto them on his left hand, Depart from me under a *curse* into the *eternal fire*." And "these shall go away into *eternal* punishment" (Matthew 25:41 and 46).

Again, listen to His words in John 3:36: "He that obeyeth not the Son shall not see life, but *the wrath of God abideth on him.*" With these quotations from Jesus' own lips, can there be any question about *the impression He meant to give?*

A Painful List

Let me add a few others to this list of heartbreaking quotations. In Acts 17:31, Paul told the Athenians, "[God] hath appointed a day in which *he will judge the world in righteousness* by the man whom he hath appointed."

He spoke plainly in Romans about those who do not repent: ". . .after thy hardness and impenitent heart treasurest up for thyself wrath in *the day of wrath* and revelation of the righteous judgment of God, who will render to every man what is due to his deed. . .unto them who are men of guile, selfishness, cunning, and obey not the truth, but obey unrighteousness, shall be *wrath* and *indignation; tribulation* and *anguish* upon every spirit of man that worketh evil" (Romans 2:5, 6, 8, and 9).

In 2 Peter 2:9, we read: "The Lord knoweth how [*i.e.*, fairly] to keep the unrighteous *under punishment*, unto the day of judgment." And in 2 Peter 3:7: "The heavens that now are, and the earth by the same word [of God as in creation] have been *stored up with fire,* being reserved against the day of judgment and destruction of ungodly men." Jude's intense little letter says this in verse 6: "Angels. . . he hath kept in everlasting bonds under *darkness* unto the judgment of the great day."

It is striking that amid Revelation's final description of Heaven's rare beauty, in stark contrast with all the surroundings, we are told: "But the cowards, and unbelieving, and abominable, and murderers, and fornicators, and dealers with demons, and worshipers of anything and anyone else than God, and all sorts of liars, *their* part shall be in the *lake of fire* and brimstone; which is the *second death*" (Revelation 21:8).

The last word is this: "*Without* are the mangy scavenger dogs, and the partners with demons. . . and everyone that doeth a lie" (Revelation 22:15). What a world of meaning is packed into one word —*without.* How alien to the vision of rare beauty in God's Homeland. Could anything be worse? Without!

That ends the list of references for now, and I am personally glad. It has been a painful task to compile them and go over them word by word.

There seem to be two stages in terms of the time and place of punishment. At *present,* these others are somewhere separated from God, in mental and spiritual anguish. We see such terms as "Gehenna," "outer darkness," and "unquenchable fire."

A second, final stage is indicated: "the lake of fire" or "the second death." Satan himself is not in Hell now, but is somewhere in the lower heavens below God's throne and above the earth (Cf. Ephesians 6:12c with Revelation 12:8). He will be cast down to the earth and later cast into the abyss, the lake of fire (Revelation 12:9, 19:20, and 20:1, 2, and 10). This is the phrase used to describe the final place for Satan and for some humans.

A program of related events is outlined. There will be a different order of things on the earth someday, lasting a long time. At its close will come a short moral crisis on the earth. Then will follow the *final disposition,* the final settlement with Satan and with any who prefer Satan's way.

The Meaning of "Torment"

An outstanding part of Jesus' teaching deals explicitly with life beyond the grave. I want to discuss it here. It is the remarkable story of the rich man and the poor beggar in Luke 16. The story is prompted by the Pharisees' criticism, and is aimed directly at them.

The Pharisees were the dominant party in Jewish politics, the official religious leaders. The church and state were the same, at that time. The Pharisees posed before the crowds as saints, but they were notoriously bad in their lives. They criticized Jesus for His friendliness to the poor, prompting the three matchless parables of Luke 15 and the parable of the unjust steward in Luke 16.

The Pharisee leaders were in the crowd listening to Jesus. His money parable stirred them. They scoffed openly, for they were *"lovers of money."* Then Jesus touched another sore spot with them by speaking of the easy divorce so common among them.

Then, immediately, He began the story of the rich man and the poor beggar. He talked first of their earthly situations. The rich man was not simply rich, but was very selfish. He lived "in mirth and splendor every day," in a constant round of lavish, selfish pleasure.

The beggar was both poor and sick. He was carried by a kind friend of his class to the rich man's gate each day, hoping for scraps. Even the dogs were kinder to him than the rich man, whose servants threw out the crumbs.

Then came the sudden change. The beggar died, ending his earthly life. The rich man died, *and was buried,* with the splendor of his life lingering over his remains; for him, too, it was the end of life on earth.

In the *next life* we see the same painful contrast between the two, but the places are exactly reversed. The beggar was carried tenderly by angels up into Abraham's bosom—the Jewish measurement of total bliss. He went by natural spirit gravity to where his spirit kinfolk were.

The rich man went to Hades. That tells us nothing of his condition until we read that he was "in *torment.*" That last word tells his story. He was not tormented because he had been rich. He moved naturally to the center of his spiritual gravity.

The word *torment* is significant. It is used four times in this story, in the Authorized Version. Two different words are underneath. The Revisions translate one of these to mean "in anguish." The rich man said, "I am in anguish in this flame." Abraham said, "Thou art in anguish."

This translation of "anguish" occurs four times in the New Testament. It occurs twice here. It is the word used for Joseph and Mary's distress when they couldn't find their son Jesus (Luke 2:48) and used by Paul's Ephesian friends at his farewell (Acts 20:38). In both cases, it is translated *sorrowing*.

Thayer's Greek Lexicon indicates these as the only occurrences of the word. Originally, it meant to cause intense pain, to be in anguish, to torment or distress yourself. It refers simply to your mental and spiritual condition.

The other word translated as *torment* here occurs in varying form twenty-two times in thirteen instances: Matthew 4:24; 8:6 and 29 (Mark 5:7, Luke 8:28); Matthew 14:24 (Mark 6:48); 18:34; Luke 16:23 and 28; 2 Peter 2:8; Revelation 9:5 (three times); 11:10; 12:2; 14:10 and 11 (twice); 18:7, 10, and 15; and 20:10. It is translated "vexed" once, "pained" or "in pain" once, "distressed" twice and some degree of "torment" eighteen times. Once, the alternate phrase "have no rest" is added, and on another occasion "sorrow."

Its original meaning refers to the testing of metals by a touchstone. It came to be used for the torture of people to make them tell the truth. The meanings of all words grow and change with usage. Notice the scriptural usage of this word.

Twice it is used for intense suffering through disease, once for the pains of childbirth, once for the difficulty of rowing in a storm, twice to describe people distressed by other people's conduct, once as a name for a jailer, once as a description by demons of their suffering, once for the pain inflicted on humans by demons, once for Satan's future suffering, once for humans' future suffering, once for Babylon's doom, and twice for the suffering of the rich man in our story. Omitting the story in Luke and the use of the word as a name for a jailer, it is used six times to describe pain within yourself, related to life's experiences; on two of these six occasions, the suffering is completely mental and spiritual.

It is used twice to describe demons suffering. Three times it describes judgmental punishment; whether this is 1) just mental and spiritual or 2) an act of God is not specified. From its usage, it seems usually to mean pain caused by one's actions or by daily experiences, not pain resulting from God's punishment.

The rich man says he is "*in anguish* in this flame." His pain, like a burning fire, is emphasized in his plea to Abraham "that he may dip his finger in water and cool my *tongue*." The language suggests a terrible thirst is burning him up.

Notice this rich man shows no change of spirit or heart. The only thing bothering him is his suffering. He does not regret the selfishness of his former life. His plea, which is perfectly natural, only seeks relief. He is sorry he is in this awful fix, but his attitude toward God hasn't changed. His afterlife is just an extension of the life he lived on earth. He is the same man, spiritually, and that seems decisive.

In Abraham's reply to his plea, two things stand out. There can be no relief by the method the rich man suggests. Furthermore, "between us and you *there's a great gulf fixed.*" It is an impassable gulf.

This is the outstanding teaching on the subject by the tenderhearted Jesus. There is another life beyond the grave. A distinction is made between humans in the next life. That distinction is shaped in the earthly life. It continues beyond the grave the way it starts here.

There is a place of incredible pain over there. The language used in the Word suggests a spiritual pain—which, of course, is the most intense kind of pain known.

There also is a place of happiness. There are humans in each place, and there is an impassable gulf between them.

In Their Own Shoes

Let me try to conclude these and related passages. A sharp distinction is drawn between two classes of humans. The distinction is based wholly on their voluntary, heartfelt attitude toward the good and pure.

At present, God is not judging us. He is letting things work out naturally. But He is keeping close watch, and a day of settlement surely is coming.

There is a place of punishment in the next life. It involves two stages. There is the present stage, running concurrently with the history of humans on earth. There is the final stage, beginning with the completely new adjustment of Heaven and Earth.

The punishment described is most intense, mentally and spiritually. Indications are that it is the intensest of all suffering. The place where this occurs is not made by God, but is created by those who stubbornly set themselves against God. Their

119

accumulated action produces the condition called Hell. That is the word used for the place where the wicked will go naturally, drawn by their spiritual gravity. God does not send anyone there. Whoever goes there goes on his or her own feet, by his or her own actions. And these individuals *stay* there.

Hell does not necessarily have a huge population, as would be concluded logically from some of the teaching on this subject. But unmistakably, there is a group of incorrigibles. The language of Scripture leads us to believe it is a small minority of incorrigibles.

Note these words, used in Revelation 20:15: "And *if any* was not found written in the book of life, he was cast into the lake of fire." The words *if* and *any* are very suggestive. It is not the language we commonly use for a great crowd, but rather for exceptional instances.

All this is heartbreaking to God. It is against His will and plan. But with utmost reverence, let me say that God cannot change these things without infringing on our freedom of action. The only way He could remove the possibility of Hell for us would be to destroy our freedom.

It might be argued that if this is so, it is a defeat for God. For surely at the end, God would be completely triumphant in saving us all. Such an argument has a very strong appeal.

Note, however, that such reasoning is not based on God's revelation but on logic, on human reasoning. Logic is very subtle. The least slip in the process spoils the conclusion. And logic is a slippery thing. One item left out, even unconsciously, ruins everything.

On the other hand, God *will* be victorious, even under the circumstances outlined here. He will hold unflinchingly to the original high standard for man: that man will be in His very own image. He will hold to it against all attacks. Man is as free in his will as God is in His.

Man is free to use his will, even while damning himself by using it in a bad way. This is complete victory for God's great love and purpose in the creation story. Meanwhile, there is clear evidence that the door of right choice is always open, although some never enter it.

This is the reasoned, logical reply. Remember that a single flaw in logic, a single omission, drastically changes the conclusion.

There is something better, more conclusive, on the other side. That fact is revealed in God's inspired Book. One citation alone contains enough evidence, even if there were no others. It is from the final view of earth's affairs. It describes God's ideal (Revelation 21:1, 22:5). Evil has met final judgment. Satan is disposed of. The old earth is replaced by a new, fully regenerated earth. There is beauty and bliss, peace and happiness.

In the middle of this lovely picture comes our abrupt citation. It is like a spot of darkest ink on whitest paper, like a mangy stray among thorough-breds. No human ever would have put this statement in that setting of bliss and purity.

Listen to the words, so out of keeping with their surroundings: "But"—*but,* a tremendous transition! —"for the fearful [or cowardly] and abominable, and murderers, and fornicators, and sorcerers [part-ners with demon spirits] and idolaters [worshipers of anything and anyone except God], and all [sorts of] liars, *their* part is in the lake that bur-neth with fire and brimstone, which is the second death" (Revelation 21:8).

That does not mean these people are known among humans as murderers, sorcerers, liars, etc., although some of them may be. It is the language of the Holy Spirit. It describes them as He sees them. (Note the blunt, honest language used by the Holy Spirit concerning the apostle Judas in John 12:6.) He sees through our motives and through life's accepted trends. Many of these would be called cultured people, moving in church circles.

The Holy Spirit, looking into their motives and inner lives, sees that *this* person is using one of his powers or talents against another human. *That* person is unclean in thoughts and acts. This *other* one is communicating with evil spirits. The one *over there* is living a lie.

"Without"

In the epilog, the same note is struck. Significantly, this time it is connected directly with the highest of all human powers, *free choice*—God's best gift to humans. Paraphrasing Revelation 22:11: "He that is set on being unrighteous, let him be free to follow his choice and do unrighteousness, and it will be with a constantly increasing momentum. And he that is set on going to the passionate depths of evildoing will be free to follow *his bent,* with the slant down getting steeper." The same thing, in the same two degrees, is said of those who choose the right way.

When Jesus comes to straighten things out, He will give to each person what the person's choices deserve (Revelation 22:12). Blessing will be pronounced on those who insist on choosing the right, regardless of difficulties and opposition, who go for the cleansing blood of the Lamb (Cf. Revelation 22:14, with 7:14).

Then immediately comes the terrible "without" sentence: "Without are those whose choice takes them there, those who do not go to be washed." The eye that sees things just as they are finds that beneath their veneers, some are spiritually like the mangy scavengers, in touch with demons, unclean; they coldly use their power to crowd others, putting their own interests above God (Revelation 22:15).

Who can speak after God has spoken? This is the last word on the subject. The ostrich shutting its eyes to danger becomes a more certain victim of the danger. We would do well not to be like the ostrich.

These are the *facts* of the matter. Later we will study the *principle* and the *process* that underlie the facts.

It has been a hard, heartrending story to tell. Yet the truth must be told simply, clearly, and in connection with related truths. To be tenderhearted without being truthful is not loving; it is unkind and cowardly.

But to tell such truth without being heartbroken by its awfulness is to be hardened, inhuman, ungodly. Jesus' most terrible denunciation of the Jewish leaders ended in a great sob (Matthew 23:37). A few days later, that sob of grief broke His heart. He made the one great, solitary sacrifice so that no one might be left outside because of sin, so that the person who chooses Him as Saviour may have full rights to the Father's house.

I sat one evening as a guest in the dining room of the Moody Bible Institute in Chicago. Mr. Moody himself sat at the head of the faculty table. After the meal a faculty member told a witty story about future punishment. It was greeted with laughter.

Instantly, Moody was on his feet. "Well," he said, "whenever you do talk about Hell, *let it be with tears in your voice.*"

Here was the rare blend of tenderness and truth that always marked Moody, and Moody's Master.

Chapter 4

Can We Communicate
With the Dead?

A True Human Instinct

It is perfectly natural to want to talk with our loved ones who have died. The fact that we cannot adds to our grief.

It is a true human instinct to miss them and to long for them intensely, to feel lonely in their absence. We may hide much of this sorrow, but any other feelings are not natural. Death is always a shock, even when it is expected. It causes a bad break.

I know a young man who, when his work took him away, wrote to his mother every day, even if it was just a few lines. When she died, it took a long time and some strange feelings for him to break that daily writing habit. He had prayed for her every day, too, and it seemed so queer not to. It seemed he was not being true to her if he didn't name her in his daily prayer. He eventually learned to put praise in place of supplication in the old-time prayer, to be thankful she was beyond trouble, up in the Master's presence. But what an impact that change of habit made!

I have a dear friend whose husband died suddenly. They had lived an ideal life together for many years. She had always leaned on his counsel and fellowship. It seemed as if she could not get used to living without him. A bit of herself had died with him.

Grief—tense, deep, overwhelming—is natural. Its emotional sweep and suction are tremendous, indescribable. It takes strong self-control to hold steady. Many fail. They are swamped. Their vision blurs, their judgment wavers, and this affects their actions.

Emotions never should be allowed to take the wheel and drive. Whenever that happens—whether the emotion is grief or joy, love or hatred—we have a runaway, with a breakdown or a smash-up ahead. The will must remain steady. It should be influenced by natural emotion, by knowledge, and by disciplined judgment, but the will must keep control.

Wartime may leave millions dead. Actual violence is joined by stress, disease, and poverty. The natural strain death puts on the living is intensified terrifically.

The Aftermath of War

It was to be expected that World War II would revive intensely the old questions about the dead, especially about whether we can communicate with the dead. The movement has swept like prairie wildfire. Under various names—spiritualism, spiritism, psychic phenomena, occultism, etc.—the old fire burns more intensely than ever, even in church pulpits.

Literature on the subject abounds. Periodicals devoted to spiritualism as a cult are profitable. A London society is said to have a three thousand-volume collection dealing with various phases of spiritism.

Mechanical ways to facilitate so-called "communication with the dead" have been in demand. One contrivance, the Ouija board, is very suggestive. The name is a loose combination of words from two languages: *oui,* French, and *ja,* German. That means "yes-yes." It will agree with anything you suggest and give you the comfortable feeling you are correct in your yearnings.

Two prominent Englishmen have led the movement. One of them visited the United States. An able physicist with cultured speech and skillful publicity, he drew great crowds. But in a survey of more than a hundred leading American scientists, educators, and psychologists, the scientific and scholarly consensus was decidedly against his teaching. Had he conducted himself so childishly in scientific circles, he never would have emerged from obscurity.

Yet we can sympathize with him to a degree, personally, while opposing his teaching. Such an emotional person with an unsteady will easily could be swept aside by the great personal grief that came to him during the war.

The other leader is a gifted and famous writer of detective stories. It is not surprising they both gained wide attention among the unthinking. Yet in neither case do the leaders' special training and achievements qualify them for sifting evidence or passing judgment on this subject. Rather, they would need to abandon their normal work and learn to examine a matter very different from their specialties.

The question of communication with the dead runs far back into the mistiest past. The present interest in it is not new.

Communication with the dead, in some form, is at the heart of nearly all the religions of the world, both civilized and savage. The two outstanding exceptions are Judaism and Christianity. Ancestor worship, or the cult of the dead, was common in early Egypt, Greece, Rome and Phoenicia, and continues in present-day China and Japan. In China, the spirit of the dead father or other kinsman is supposed to enter the ancestral tablet and commune with living relatives. The ancestor supposedly helps and protects the living relatives. A slavish fear underlies this ancestor worship.

In its higher forms, ancestor worship is an abnormal, morbid extension of respect for one's parents and elders. It becomes an improper exaggeration of a perfectly normal thing. It degenerates into its lower form of communication with spirits, witchcraft, and the like. Respect degenerates into fear.

Three Groups

Can we communicate with the dead? Some insist we can. They teach that spirits of the dead *do* come back to us and try to communicate, and the problem is that we and the spirits are in two different spheres. So, they say, there is a natural difficulty, like the difficulty between people who speak different languages until the new language is learned.

These teachers fall into three groups. At the lowest level are those who believe *in ghosts*. They usually are ignorant and superstitious, though it is surprising how common this is among all classes. The ghosts are supposed to be spirits of humans who have died and who return to their former homes. One strange feature of this belief is the terrible sense of fear that goes with it, as though death has changed the character of the loved ones into harmful beings.

I recall a sensible remark made by a simple man living in the country. Terror had seized some locals because the ghost of a recently deceased kinsman was thought to have come back. "Well," he said, "if he's in Hell he can't come back, and if he's in Heaven he doesn't want to come back." But such logic is too rare.

Then there are the *professionals,* known as mediums, who make a living by claiming to communicate with the dead. They supposedly supply the medium of communication between the two worlds. Mediums are found in many cities. Sometimes they are called *clairvoyants,* referring to those who can see clearly. The word is a French derivative, as is the word *séance,* which means a sitting or a session.

The third group is supposed to be on a higher level. It consists of the so-called *scientific investigators*. They profess to base the whole thing on science or study. A common phrase they use is "psychical research." Related to this is the study of hypnotism, mesmerism, magnetism, etc.

Without doubt, this is a legitimate, broad field for research, but some of these investigators tend to drop to the lower levels. It is rather surprising how some intelligent people who insist on rigid evidence in other fields are more accepting in their ghostly research. The British Society for Psychical Research has had on its rolls the names of many distinguished publicists and prominent individuals from various backgrounds, but its activities seem to be controlled by a certain group who lean toward the results they are eager to find.

An Uncharted Realm of Mental Science

There is a legitimate kind of psychical research within the realm of psychology. There are certain functions of the mind that don't seem to be fully understood or defined.

Psychology, as taught in textbooks and schools, conventionally has ignored these functions. That is one extreme. The psychical specialists who try to treat the subject in a scholarly way usually do not make clear analyses. That is the other extreme.

There seem to be mental traits, gifts, or functions that should be included in our natural mental powers but have been lost, or partly lost, through sin. Some still have these gifts, to some extent, but they seem uncanny to the ordinary person.

These functions are said to belong to the subconscious. That is, they work while we are unconscious of them. They also are said to be subliminal, below the threshold of consciousness. The thought is the same with both terms.

For instance, a person will have a premonition about a loved one far away, or about some coming event. Without doubt, the Holy Spirit guides those in touch with Him regarding such things. But in addition to this guidance is a mental trait that triggers the premonition. This trait is accented in some; in others it seems completely missing.

A close friend of mine has this sort of mental quality to a high degree. For instance, it comes to him that someone will call or will act in a certain detailed way, and that's the way it turns out. He has driven along country roads and envisioned places, people, and incidents; then maybe two or three miles down the road, he has come across exactly what his spirit vision has seen.

He is an earnest Christian, somewhat familiar with the dangers we are discussing here. He follows the settled principle of not trying to tamper with an unfamiliar realm, but prayerfully to subject all his powers to the Holy Spirit's constant guidance.

Remarkably, he constantly experiences a strong impulse to pray for a certain person, as if the person who comes to mind is in need or danger or temptation. Repeatedly, he learns later of the actual need, danger, or special temptation, and of the deliverance.

If you possess some such gift, you should pray quietly about it. Dedicate it, with *all* your powers, to the Master. Never try to use it except by the Holy Spirit's gracious guidance, in practical ways. Be especially cautious, because the gift is not understood clearly.

Similar to this is the experience of certain saintly people as they near death's door. The veil between this life and the spirit world seems to grow thinner. As their physical powers weaken, the spirit vision seems to be able to see new things.

As Stephen stood amid the raging, murderous mob, the eyes of his spirit were opened. He saw beyond the range of physical eyesight. What did he see? Jesus!—glorified, standing at the Father's right hand (Acts 7:55).

I remember the light that came into the face of a dear saint as she was slipping over into the King's presence. She looked up quietly, intently, as though she could see someone or something we could not see. Her eyes and face beamed. She looked at those around her bed as if to say, "Can't you see, too?" Then she sank into the sleep that carried her into the presence of the Lord she loved so much.

The word *telepathy* has been coined for something related to this: the unusual communication of one person with another of like mind. One mind seems to communicate with another without words, looks or gestures. Some are very sensitive to this.

Our ignorance of these uncommon mental traits or powers has been used skillfully by experts who themselves are sensitive in this regard and have cultivated their sensitivity. These professional spiritualists are apt to blend subtly the legitimate with the illegitimate in cunning trickery. The uninformed, perhaps during the stress of some great grief, is swept away.

Responses Do Come

These are the three groups of people who answer yes to our question. They say there *is* a response to their efforts to communicate. And let me state that *there are responses,* without question.

But please note keenly *the character of these responses*. Without exception, they are vague, indefinite, and insufficient, and they frequently are childish. They can be taken to mean different things. They sometimes are dovetailed shrewdly into suggestions made by the medium.

If these responses indeed were communicated from our dead loved ones, it would be rather disheartening. It would indicate those we loved have lost many of their mental powers. They lack their former common sense.

The critical question is *where do these responses come from?* The spiritists or mediums say they come from the spirits of our dead loved ones. Some psychologists who specialize in the psychic nature of things say they come from within ourselves, from our subconsciousness.

After long, careful, prayerful study, I concluded there are only *five possible sources* from which they may come. The experts say they indeed come from our dead loved ones.

They may come from a subtle interplay between the inner working of two human minds: the mind of the inquirer and the mind of the professional. (That would make it wholly mental!) They may come through the expert's cunning deception of an overly emotional inquirer, or through the expert's dealing with an uneducated, gullible inquirer or observer. They may come from demons. Or they may come through a subtle mixture of two or more of these. I am certain that all five sources must be considered, and that they cover all the ground.

The English friend who lectured so widely in the United States is reported to have stated, in effect, that *the fact of a response* established that there is communication with the dead loved one. It seems incredible that a man of his intelligence could have made such a claim. It childishly ignores the various possible sources of the responses.

I have arrived at my personal conviction about where these responses come from after weighing everything carefully. I have read ghost stories and related literature. I have talked in America and Europe with sensible people who have had unusual experiences. I have tried to examine the Psychical Research Society and related literature. Although I never have attended a séance, as a matter of principle, I have talked with people who have.

I have reached three conclusions. First, human spirits do *not* return to talk with us; there is never communication with them. Second, haunted houses, apparitions, and the like can be explained fully either by the presence of demons or by our subtler mental processes (subjective impressions, hallucinations, etc.).

Third, the responses that come through spiritistic experts are never messages from the dead. Some of them are from demons, whose purpose we will see momentarily. Some are the subtle, unconscious mental interplay between the inquirer and the medium. And some are merely *deliberate, skillful deception* by the medium.

It is very interesting to examine the conditions these experts say are essential for good results. Most significantly, they say the inquirer should have an uncritical, undoubting spirit. The inquirer should be passive and sympathetic. The more fully you can give up all self-control and yield wholly to the expert's influences, the better the results.

The Authoritative Answer

But we don't have our answer yet. The authoritative answer is yet to come—and it *is* authoritative.

When we get it, there is no more to be said. It is the answer found in the Book of God. The Book recognizes this question, discusses it fully, and answers it flatly and positively.

The Bible is an index to the moral customs and conditions of the nations surrounding the old Jewish nation (which means practically all the nations of the Biblical world, for the Jewish domain lay at its center, touched directly or indirectly by all the nations). Every national culture influenced its life, and in later centuries every civilization marched its armies over that territory. The prohibitions contained in the Ten Commandments, and the numerous detailed prohibitions grouped with them, became a perfect mirror reflecting the common moral conditions of the surrounding nations.

From the earliest times, all these nations had a class of experts in the cult of the dead, the foretelling of the future, the settling of difficult questions, the interpreting of dreams, and, generally, the magical and mysterious. Practically, this was the priestly class, for this sort of thing was connected with their religion, and constituted a large part of it. (See Genesis 41:8; Exodus 7:11 and 22; 8:7; Daniel 2:2, 10, and 27; and 4:6 and 7.) This class of professionals flourished at various times among the Jews, though expressly prohibited (1 Samuel

15:23; 28:3 and 8–15; 2 Kings 21:6; and 23:24).

The various names for these magical experts are significant. An index is given in Moses' farewell talks in the Plains of Moab (Deuteronomy 18:9–14). "There shall not be found with thee anyone that maketh his son or daughter to *pass through the fire,* one that *useth divination,* one that practices *augury,* or an *enchanter,* or a *sorcerer,* or a *charmer,* or a *consulter with a familiar spirit,* or a *wizard,* or a *necromancer.*"

These are grouped as one class, all abominable to God, with nine different names, according to the methods they used or the pretensions they made. Then the whole class is categorized under two names: augury and diviners.

The necromancer was one who consulted with the dead and divined or foretold by that means. The name used for another of these sheds light on the whole class: "a consulter with a *familiar spirit.*" "Familiar spirit" is the old English term for the Devil or demon. The pretended purpose of these experts was communication with the dead. The *real* purpose was communication with demons or evil spirits. In other words, all this was *devilcraft,* as the Holy Spirit reveals plainly here. Other names sometimes are used for the same general craft: astrologers, stargazers, monthly prognosticators, soothsayers (Isaiah 47:12, 13; Jeremiah 27:9, 10).

One thing is emphasized: All of this sort of thing was forbidden by God, in the strongest language. It was characterized as the worst sort of wickedness, to be punished in the extreme.

One passage stands out as an index to related passages. It was spoken to Israel at a time when the nation was deep in spiritual decline: "And when they shall say unto you, seek unto them that have familiar spirits [demons] and unto the wizards that chirp, and that mutter: should not a people seek unto their *God? Should they seek unto the dead on behalf of the living?* To the teaching and testimony [of God's Word]! If they speak not according to this word, surely there is no morning [no dawning, no hope] for them" (Isaiah 8:19, 20).

That's pretty plain talk. And it applies especially to life today!

These devilcrafters worked aggressively, but it was a time of distress in the nation. The people sorely needed guidance. What would they do? The answer was simple: Go to God's Book. It has plain teaching. It will tell you. If you do not heed, things will go badly for you, sooner or later.

Listen to these three passages spoken by *God Himself* and recited by Moses with the Ten Commandments:

"Thou shalt not suffer a sorceress to live" (Exodus 22:18).

"Ye shall not use enchantments, nor practice augury. . . . Turn ye not unto them that have familiar spirits [demons], nor unto the wizards; seek them not out, to be defiled by them. I am Jehovah your God" (Leviticus 19:26, 31).

"The soul that turneth unto them that have familiar spirits [demons], and unto the wizards, to play the harlot after them, I will even set my face against that soul, and will cut him off from among his people. . . . A man or a woman that hath a familiar spirit [demon] or that is a wizard, shall surely be put to death; they shall be stoned with stones" (Leviticus 20:6, 27).

Could stronger language be used? These practices were defiling, morally dirty. They were classed with the worst sort of sexual impurity, extremely alien to God. They were to be punished by one of the most drastic forms of death—stoning.

Another stinging example comes from the lips of Samuel. If anyone in this old Book could use plain, stinging language, it was Samuel. He is talking to King Saul. Listen, and watch Saul's face whiten under the rebuke: "Rebellion [that is, simply failure to obey God] is as witchcraft [devil-craft], and stubbornness [being set in your own way against God's way] is extreme iniquity and devil worship" (1 Samuel 15:23). In other words, these occult, magical practices are extremely evil, devilish. Samuel uses the superlative degree.

These things become the touchstone of the worst wickedness. National reformations hit directly at them (1 Samuel 28:3, 9; 2 Kings 23:24, et al). Bad kings revived them (2 Kings 21:6, 2 Chronicles 33:6). Because of these and related practices, the Canaanite nations were cast out and, much later, Israel went to pieces (2 Kings 16:3, 17:7). They are referenced repeatedly in the prophets' denunciations (Isaiah 19:3; 29:4; 44:25; Jeremiah 27:9, 10; Micah 3:6, 7, 11; Malachi 3:5).

With these sharp words from the Old Testament in mind, turn to the other end of the Book. Paul in his old age, his spirit vision sensitized by the Holy Spirit's touch, discerned that at the end of the Church Age, "some [in the church] shall fall away from the [true] faith, giving heed to seducing [misleading] demons, and to things taught by demons through pretended good men who really speak lies, and whose consciences are seared as with a hot iron" (1 Timothy 4:1 and 2).

The Evil Purposes Underneath

No teaching from God's Word could be plainer. Attempted communication with the dead is allied directly with the worst black art. It is grouped with devilcraft. It is dealing with demons. It is a distinctly forbidden realm, expressly and strongly prohibited. Such practices are characterized as defiling, abominable, subject to extreme punishment.

But there is even more than this to be learned. Note the *utter incompetence* of such attempts to produce what we desire. There simply is not and cannot be communication with our loved ones who have gone. Pretensions of this sort are deceiving.

The fact that there are such pretensions, made so positively and aggressively, becomes significant. There clearly is a purpose behind them, an evil purpose—indeed, the purpose of the Evil One himself. He is behind it.

And *his purpose* is plain as it is brazen and startling. *He wants to get control of humans.* He can get control only by our consent, either given freely or extracted by deception. Demoniacs are extreme instances of Satan's control. They are humans so completely possessed that they have lost *all* self-control.

They actually are too demon-controlled to be useful to the Devil. They have gotten out of *his control*. Demoniacs are described in the Gospels, and they can be found today, though their families often are ashamed to have the fact known.

In the western world, uncontrollable cases of demon possession mostly are found in mental institutions. Some of these have gone too far to be of use to the Evil One. He prefers just enough control to use the person in normal, daily life, mingling among others.

The danger of tampering with this kind of thing is terribly real. I remember a small book I came across years ago. It discussed the serious dangers of these practices. It was not written from the Christian standpoint—in fact, just the opposite, which made it warnings more pointed. The writer apparently was not concerned with the question of right or wrong, only with the danger to one's mentality and self-control. Those who attempt to communicate with the spirit world, he wrote, *"open a door that by and by they cannot shut, when they earnestly want to shut it."* He described cases with disastrous results.

Even the English author and lecturer previously referred to warns his audiences against the dangers of spiritist experiments. This is very significant.

I remember a North German peasant I knew years ago. Honest, eager, and simplehearted, he had been plainly demon-possessed, against his will. Happily, through prayer and instruction, he was set free.

I was struck by his unusually clear explanation of how his trouble came: "I was ignorant of the danger; I opened the door; the evil spirit came in; and I couldn't free myself of his presence."

These examples illustrate the terrible dangers of tampering with such things.

The Witch of Endor

I want to discuss two passages which, at first, may seem surprising. There are two, and only two instances in the Bible of communication with the dead. They clearly were planned by God Himself, and they are very different from the Devil's kind of communication.

The first is the case of Samuel and the witch of Endor (1 Samuel 28:3–19). Look at it briefly. King Saul, who sought the witch's help, is *out of touch with God.* That is an outstanding feature of the story. He twice has disobeyed openly God's explicit commands. And he is the national leader, which makes a bad thing much worse. Whatever he does, the crowds will do (1 Samuel 13:8–14, 15:1–23).

In an emergency (it is always an emergency that tempts us so strongly), Saul seeks an illegitimate means of guidance. He himself has forbidden witch-craft under penalty of death. Now, disguised, he secretly travels north by night to Endor to consult a witch. He calms her fear for her own safety in doing this prohibited thing, and asks her to summon Samuel, who has been dead for some time.

Remarkably, Samuel does come and talk with Saul. But obviously *the witch has nothing to do with Samuel's coming.* Instead, she is astonished. The whole incident is taken out of her hands. To her fright, a spirit actually comes before her eyes. She instantly recognizes him as Samuel, the nation's great, longtime leader, and it shocks her. The ordinary translation of the King James Version and the Revisions reports that "she cried with a loud voice." A fuller, accurate translation would be: "She was greatly startled and gave out suddenly a piercing shriek of distress."

This is the first thing to note—that the witch has nothing to do with Samuel's coming. This is a new experience for her, an unwelcome experience. Something is happening totally outside her realm.

The second thing to notice is the sharp contrast between this communication from Samuel and other so-called communications from the dead. The latter are characteristically vague, cryptic, ambivalent, or notably beneath the intelligence of the person who is supposed to be speaking, and they try to leave an agreeable impression.

Here, Samuel speaks in his old way. He gives definite, detailed information of a very unwelcome nature about the tragic happenings that will occur tomorrow. Saul will be defeated by the Philistines, will lose the kingdom and will die, along with his sons. This is a stinging rebuke.

Mark carefully the influence of this incident on the impressionable Hebrews. The occurrence could not be hid. The grapevine took it to every corner of Israel. It was the talk of the nation. *And* it was a setback for witchery and similar practices.

An awe or fear came over the people. They were afraid to attempt this sort of thing again. God had rebuked it. It is the only incident of its type in the Old Testament.

The other exceptional incident is the appearance of Moses on the Mount of Transfiguration (Matthew 17:1–8, and parallels). I refer to it only because it is an instance of communication with the dead. Obviously, it belongs to a different realm of discussion, a higher realm.

Moses had died sixteen centuries earlier. Now he plainly appears, along with Elijah, the fiery denouncer of witchery and devilcraft. Moses' identity is recognized immediately. He talks with our Lord Jesus. And he talks on a subject that is especially obnoxious to the Devil and to every practitioner of the black arts: the sacrificial death of Jesus on the cross.

These are the two exceptions in the Book. They reiterate the Book's prohibitions of devilcraft and its allied arts. God deemed it wise, for practical purposes, to have these occurrences be recorded. In both cases, *He* took the *initiative*.

Meeting Our Human Need

The question of praying for the dead is very interesting. It is at the other end of this subject—we're not seeking help *from* the dead, but are trying to help them.

The custom of praying for the dead has been part of the church, to varying extents, since the second century. It is common in some churches today.

Only one passage of Scripture is quoted to support it: 2 Timothy 1:18. But that statement supposed Onesiphorus was dead—which was possible but not at all certain. The utter silence of Scripture on the subject, apart from this doubtful passage, would seem significant.

We are not told to pray for the dead. If our loved ones are in the Lord's presence, prayer seems needless. If not, aren't they past the influence of prayer? We will discuss this later more fully. Meanwhile, praise can take the place of supplication when the names of our dear ones come to our lips at prayer time.

Grief is epidemic. Hearts are sore and bleeding. The home is a lonely place for many. Mealtime brings heartbreaking memories. Loneliness eats into some of us like acid. We hunger for fellowship. We need clear guidance in our everyday affairs. We want to know about our loved ones. Can we find no help, when the rain of grief bears down on us day and night?

There is an answer to these heartfelt cries. It is immediate, plain, complete, and human. There is a Friend who will share your lonely corner and fill it and you with warmth and glad singing.

This Friend is real. He has a human touch. He knows all about things down here. He knows what it is like to lose a dear friend unexpectedly. There is not one experience down here that He does not know (except experiences that come through wrong choices).

So He *can* tell you what to do in emergencies and tight corners. And He *will*. Moreover, He is as closely in touch with your loved one as with you. He is your connecting link.

What do I mean? Whom am I talking about? Listen, while I try to bypass the hard shell of familiar words to the throbbing realities inside them. He is the Holy Spirit. He understands all that Jesus went through.

There is more. He is the Spirit of the glorified, enthroned Jesus. He knows all our true human feelings *and* He knows all the divine power. He is truly God, as well as human. His coming to live in you is real. He *speaks* in this Book of God. He spoke in it long ago, and He will talk to you through its pages today. He will talk directly to your inner spirit. He will surround you with His presence.

Getting in Touch

But, you say, *how* can He become real to me? The answer is simple but radical: Surrender yourself to the Lord Jesus as *Master* as well as Saviour. Surrender constantly.

Please Him. In a sane, wholesome way, make this the focus of your daily life. Put His Word above all other reading. Spend some *quiet time* alone with it each day. Drink it in. Breathe in its spirit. Absorb it. Brood over it.

Learn to spend the day with God. He is with you, and in you, in the Person of His Holy Spirit. Thank Him for His presence. Do it daily. Sing Him songs of praise, regularly. Talk to Him even when you don't need to ask for something. Practice His presence. He is there by your side as you are reading this.

This sort of thing will discipline your judgment. You will want to know the meaning of "watch and pray." You will learn to watch for the subtle, crafty enemy who masquerades these days in his "angel of light" costume, with smooth voice and reverent bearing. You must learn to pray with one eye open.

In practicing His presence, you must balance wholesome sanity, trained vision, and disciplined judgment.

You may be one of those dear people who think this does not help you a bit, for you are not in touch with God. Your mind is tormented with doubts about God and His Word, about this whole discussion. Well, here is something for you, *if you are honest* (the first essential). Listen. My honestly skeptical friend can get a *direct response from God to his or her own soul,* if it truly is desired. A pierced Hand is on your doorknob right now. Someone is waiting at your doorstep to come in. And He will give you a *response* that will *satisfy* your deepest longings.

A mother with a troubled face spoke to John Bartholomew Gough at the close of his famous temperance lectures. She had a darling, grown son who called himself a skeptic. The mother's heart was breaking. Would Mr. Gough talk with her boy?

They met. The young man poured out his doubts. He seemed really sincere. Gough listened as a friend, and finally said, "Why don't you pray? Prayer is a natural thing."

But to whom should he pray? He did not think there was a God.

Gough said, "Why not pray to Love? You believe in love. You believe in your dear mother's love for you. That is a pure, holy passion."

That touched a sensitive spot. The young man said he would pray to that.

In his bedroom that night, the man knelt with closed eyes and cried out passionately, "O Love!" Instantly, softly, the words seemed to come to his inner being: "God is Love."

The man impulsively cried out, "O God!" Again, so softly, were spoken to him the words he already knew by heart: "God so loved the world that he gave his only begotten."

Again, yielding to the quick impulse in his spirit, his lips cried out, "O Christ!"

And at once, something came. An exquisite sense of peace stole into his spirit as he knelt. The *fog of doubt*—where had it gone? A thousand questions remained unanswered, *but* there was a singular, quiet sense of peace within. He was *in touch* with Him who made peace by the blood of the cross.

Anybody who wants to can get in touch. The Man who was killed for us is now within reach. The honest heart reaching can get in touch. And that touch *with Him* will answer all questions and needs.

Chapter 5

What Is Death?

Pleasing, but not True

Death means death of the body. That is the biggest thing we understand, the thing we feel most.

The body we loved so much lies lifeless under the sod. We do not see it. The loved one is absent. The spirit that looked out from the eyes is gone. The break between body and spirit is complete. This person is dead. The separation between us seems complete.

That common meaning of death is accurate, as far as it goes. But it is limited. It absorbs us—but there is more. We want to talk practically about that "more."

One common teaching of death is directly opposite to Biblical teaching. It belittles death to the point of practically ignoring it. Death is pictured as a mere transition, a natural step from one state of existence to another. Death is not an enemy, not a thing to be feared.

This teaching is marked by vague looseness. There are no clear, careful definitions of death. In their place are partial truths expressed in beautiful language, but blurry. Choice bits of literature have found their way into Christian circles. Death is likened to certain changes of development in the natural order. The caterpillar passes into chrysalis form and ultimately emerges as a rare, beautiful butterfly. Death is like that, according to this teaching.

Death is presented as a simple transition, a part of nature. This is acceptable to many if not most people. They like the analogy. But it entirely ignores certain *facts*. It opposes the plain teaching of the Book of God. It tends to blur the fact that the time of death is a time of moral adjustment. This adjustment hinges on our choices and on our character.

This teaching belittles or ignores what Jesus did for us when He died. It keeps us from emphasizing our choice of Christ as Saviour. It lulls us into a sort of fool's paradise where everything is all right with us, regardless of how we have lived or what we have believed.

The Meaning Pictured

Now I want to turn to the book. It is striking to find in its very opening pages a definition of death.

It is a pictured definition. That makes it easy for us all to understand. Everyone loves to look at a picture. And when a skilled artist points out the colorings, lights, shades, groupings, and postures, it is fascinating.

Look at this picture. It is in a garden. The man's friendly God is walking through the garden, side by side with him. They are friends together. The man's Friend is showing him around his new garden home. They stop under a tree. And the Friend says clearly, "In the day thou eatest thereof thou shalt surely die" (Genesis 2:17).

It is the tree of choice that will determine their continued companionship. God is pleading for the man to make the *right* choice. Their fellowship is the plea. God is saying, as father to son, "Let us always be in closest touch."

But it is for the man to decide. By making the right choices constantly, he will become like God in character and wisdom.

That is the first reference to death. The actual phrase is: "Dying, thou shalt die." There is a beginning, a process, and a finished result.

Then comes the temptation story, with the yielding to temptation and the break in fellowship. Note what "die" actually means to these two kinfolk of ours. They eat the forbidden fruit and at once are conscious of some difference in themselves. They become self-conscious about their bodies for the first time. Something seems wrong to them, for they do something to change their appearance.

The only change in them is mental or spiritual. The forbidden act makes this change. They are separated in spirit from God. Things are not the same between them.

Then comes a second step. They try to hide from God. Already they misunderstand Him. They think because they cannot see Him, He cannot see them. They want to get away from God.

The separation between them and God is increasing by this action. There is no difference in God, but the humans long to be separated from Him. That means there *is* a separation *in spirit,* widened by their desire to leave His presence.

Then comes the third stage in the separation process. They are driven out of the immediate, conscious presence of God. Although the driving out almost certainly is a moral issue, their sense of God's presence now influences them to leave His presence voluntarily.

Then comes the awful break in the home. That inner spirit that wanted to separate from God in the garden grows strong and passionate in the home of Adam and Eve. It leads Cain to seek a forced separation from one whose presence he has come to hate.

The final stage in this picture of death occurs some nine hundred years later, when it is said of Adam, "and he died." God had said, *"In the day* thou eatest thereof, dying, thou shalt die." The dying began on that day, but bodily death was postponed more than nine hundred years.

No Change in God

Plainly, death here means spiritual separation from God. It has a beginning. It is a process that intensifies in character. It is a final result. It immediately affects the man's spirit toward God, and ultimately it affects his body.

The hold of the human spirit on the body in which it lives is affected. Bodily conditions are affected. This worsens until the spirit and body no longer can hold together. The spirit's separation from God comes to include bodily conditions.

Notice there is no change in action or attitude on God's part. The separation grieves Him. He continues His creative, sustaining touch as far as He is allowed. The separation is wholly on man's part, in his spirit and his will. Man *wants* to get away. That finally results in the full separation that eventually brings bodily death.

Death is unnatural. It clearly was not in the original plan. It could not be. It results directly from man breaking with God. At the core, death is this separation from God. Life is full contact with God. Death is the reverse. If an electric wire is cut, the current cannot get through.

Notice the two stages of death. One is immediate: the inner, spiritual attitude toward God. Change occurs with the break from God, and God calls it death.

The second stage, death to the body, does not come until later. It is really less than our spiritual break, though it is the big thing, as humans see it. The more serious break by the inner spirit happens immediately and increases its influence.

Here, then, is the pictured definition of death. It is the reverse of life. Life is full touch of the spirit or heart with God. Any break in that touch means the loss of life, in some measure, and that is called death.

Death grows. It moves from one stage to a deeper one. It eventually includes bodily death, which is the main thing from the human perspective, but not from the Biblical perspective.

This is the meaning of death throughout this Book of God. Given at the very beginning, it clearly sets the standard of meaning throughout the Bible.

Tracing the Trail

Now thoughtfully run through the Book. It is impossible to quote the long string of passages, but we can follow the trail of the definition. It is an easy trail to follow. And when we have followed it to the end, another run-through brings the countless illustrations to our attention. The separation of spirit, defined as the crucial feature, colors the narrative from end to end.

Death is the separation of one's spirit from God. It affects one's spirit at once, and with a growing intensity. It affects one's body at once imperceptibly; this change increases gradually until the body loses contact with the human spirit that inhabits it (Matthew 8:22; Luke 15:24, 32; Romans 8:6; Ephesians 2:1, 5; 5:14; 1 Timothy 5:6; Revelation 3:1).

Death is the immediate, logical outcome of sin. It

does not result from arbitrary action on God's part. Sin is the beginning of death. Death is sin in its final, finished shape. To express the verb *to sin* grammatically: present tense, *to sin;* first future tense, *to suffer;* second future tense, *death.* The pliable verb becomes a hardened noun (Romans 5:12; 6:21 and 23).

Death is not just bodily death (1 Timothy 5:6; Revelation 3:1; Ephesians 2:1, 5; and 5:14), though, of course, it includes that. It is not ceasing to exist; the spirit never ceases to exist. The rich man still lived (quite possibly against his will) after his body was dead (Luke 16:19–31). And death is not a form of sleep, for the spirit never sleeps, as shown in the same reference.

Being a break in the natural order, death is painful. It is natural to dread death and shrink from it. Death is an enemy, an intruder. That word *enemy* sums up the whole case here (1 Corinthians 15:26).

Death, from its beginning to its end, passes through three stages. The first is the spiritual break with God, the rupture of friendship or fellowship with Him. Man was made for fellowship with God, but whether he would remain in that state depended on his desires, choices, and actions (Genesis 2:17, with most of the quotations already cited). God eagerly longs for that fellowship, but only when it is given freely.

This first stage of death begins at once with a wrong choice. It is spiritual death, and it goes to the root of our relationship with God. It puts the dry rot of death into the seed of life. It is death by suicide. Man cuts himself off from the source of his life. It means separation from God, separation of spirit and heart. This reveals the enormity of what Christ must do when the time comes; He has to make a whole new start (John 3:3–6).

The second stage, death of the body, is what looms so large to the human mind. The break between the human spirit and its body becomes complete. The spiritual break with God now affects the body in the extreme.

This is the least part of death. It is the temporary stage. This stage is for believers and nonbelievers alike, until Christ comes again. Then will come a change for those in touch with Him.

The third stage is the final, permanent stage. It is not for all. It is only for those who incorrigibly insist on leaving out God and Christ. It is called "the second death." The first death is the spiritual death; this is that same spiritual death, in its final, hardened form (Revelation 2:11; 20:6, 14; 21:8).

Five Things Jesus Did

This makes us see what a desperate task Jesus undertook. In dealing with dead humans, the only way to do it was to begin a new life within. In the beginning it was simply a matter of creation. Now a new creation is required, with the wreck of the old one to be cleared away.

Mankind was enslaved to Satan (Romans 6:16). That slavery had to be broken. But death was the stamp of slavery, Satan's mark of control. Death therefore had to be put to death, and Satan had to be throttled.

Sin, during the course of human history, became a slander on God's character and on God's management of the world. God had let things run in their own bad way, instead of clearing them up all at once, as He could have done.

We must understand what sort of God He is, and why He let things run on without prompt settlement. Our separation from Him hardened our hearts against Him. The hardening worsened. Our spiritual death penetrated deep within our hearts.

Now, hush your hearts and look reverently at what Jesus did. First, He got in touch with us humans. He lived a simple, true, human life, with ordinary work and temptations, for thirty years—most of His life on earth. He really was one of us, but He kept in full touch with the Father in daily life.

Then He voluntarily gave up His life for us. He took upon Himself the death that should have been ours, both bodily death and the deeper, more bitter spiritual death caused by our separation from the Father. That is the meaning of His heart-breaking cry, "Why didst thou forsake me?" He took upon Himself *all* that was coming to us.

He went down into the jaws of death, into the belly of Hell. There, he put Death to death. He throttled it beyond reviving. By dying Himself, He annihilated the power of him who has the power of death, the Devil himself (Hebrews 2:14). Having done that, He quietly rose out of death's domain, back toward the true center of gravity of His own life.

When He came up, He brought something price-less with Him. He brought up life, His own life, a new kind of deathless life that never can be tainted by death. He brought it up into plain view for all to see, so we can make our choice, accepting Him as Saviour, Redeemer, and Master (2 Timothy 1:10).

So he settled our score, set us free from our

slavery to sin, gave us a new, eternal life, vindicated God's patient endurance of sin's havoc, and broke our hearts with His indescribable love. Now, anybody who will get in touch of heart with Christ will escape death's separation from God and receive full life (John 3:16; 5:21, 24; 8:51; 11:25).

Freedom from the lesser stage of death, bodily death, is not promised. But in its place we are promised a rising up from the grave for our bodies, even as He rose (John 6:39, 40, 44, and 54). And something greater is promised. Our spirits will have such a victory over our dark, fearsome enemy death that when it does come to our bodies, we will greet it with a joyous shout (1 Corinthians 15:55–57). Meanwhile, we have the glad hope that His return to earth will spare us from that last touch with our old enemy.

But Jesus does even more. He is not through with death yet. Twice we are told He has "abolished death" (1 Corinthians 15:25, 26 (revised); 2 Timothy 1:10). He has made it inoperative, put it out of action.

Taken together, these scriptural passages mean three things. They mean spiritual death is abolished for all whose hearts come in touch with Jesus. They mean during the kingdom time, actual death (bodily death) will cease on earth (1 Corinthians

15:25, 26), probably gradually.

The third meaning is this: There will be a final abolition of death for all, at the end of things on earth (Revelation 21:4). All, that is, *except* Satan and anyone who incorrigibly insists on going Satan's way (Revelation 20:14, 15; 21:8).

Death is put to death for all who want it to be. It is this way only because Christ suffered what we are spared.

Chapter 6

Is There Another Chance
for Salvation After Death?

Four Common Answers

This is a question of chances. It will be a sober, thoughtful study. We believe everyone should have a fair chance, there should be "fair play." That is really the underlying question here. Will everyone have a "fair chance" and receive "fair play"?

That is to say, is God fair? Will He *be* fair with us when the judgment comes? Some have said God may *not* give an individual a fair chance. Are they right or wrong?

A chance is an opportunity. So it is a question of *opportunity*. If you examine that, it is really a question of a person's *use* of opportunity. Look just a bit deeper and you will see it is a matter of holding onto our *ability* to use the opportunity.

This directly touches one of the automatic laws of life: What we do not use we lose. What we can do but do not do, eventually we lose the power to do. Failure to perform steals our power to perform. If you refuse to use your eyes, if you stay in the dark, ultimately you will lose your power to see. If you do not use any given set of muscles, they waste away, and you won't be able to use them when you want to.

So the real question is this: Will the person who has not used the opportunity to make the right choice on earth be given another opportunity? Will the present opportunity extend beyond the grave? Or if an individual has not *used* his or her opportunity here, will the power to use it exist over there?

Everyone is master of his or her own destiny. You make your own life. Your present action controls your future. Everyone is a prince or princess. God said at the beginning for us to "have dominion" or mastery. You are a master. You are masterful in your actions. You were made that way.

So it may be said that *life is opportunity*. I want to say this as strongly as I can: The biggest single feature of life is that it is an opportunity. If you are alive, you have the opportunity to choose, to refuse, to go up or down. The earth is uniquely the place of opportunity, an open door to everyone on it.

Is this the reason there is such a terrific moral battle on earth? Is this why the Evil One seems to be massing all his forces *now* and *here?* The earth obviously is a battlefield, a great moral battlefield. Every human's life is a battlefield. The battle of earth is fought and settled on the human battlefield of a person's life.

Is there *another* chance? The emphasis is on the word *another*. Is there another chance after our life on earth?

There are four common answers to this question.

Some say we do not need another chance. No matter how we have used or not used our chance here, we all will pull through on the other side, past any dangers. Some even think we all will pull through easily.

Then there are growing numbers who say positively, "Yes, there *is* another chance." Different groups hold this view.

Strangely, there are two separate "no" answers, from two groups aggressively opposed to each other. Some say, "No, there is not another chance because if you have not used your chance here, that is the end of you. You simply cease to exist. There is no other chance for you because there is no 'you' left to have another chance." This teaching is called *conditional immortality*. Immortality, or continued existence, is conditioned on our relationship to Christ, it says.

The second "no" group gives the same general answer, but from a radically different angle. This is the so-called *orthodox* group. Instead of another chance, there is an endless time of sleepless remorse over the unused chance. Pain never stops cutting into your increasingly sensitive spirit, they say. The flame never burns out. Theirs is a plain, blunt "no," sometimes stated harshly.

The True Answer

What is *the true answer?* Is there an *authoritative* answer?

Yes, there is. There is an authoritative Book, and *it* gives the one authoritative answer. It is the one source of *reliable information.* What we need is not opinion, theory, or wish. The matter is too serious. We must know authoritatively, *if* that is possible. Happily, it is. The Book of God gives the clear, positive answer.

Let me give the Book's answer in a single sentence. Then we will turn to the Book for specific statements. Surprisingly, it does not agree directly with any of the above four answers, although it comes to mean practically the same as one of them.

The Book's answer is *yes and no.* As far as the character of God's love is concerned, there is another chance that seemingly never runs out. As far as a human's decision is concerned, there is no other chance. And our decision is the determining factor there, just as it is here. That seems to be the Book's authoritative answer.

Now look into the Book for its detailed teachings.

The first question to be examined is this: *Is death the dividing line of opportunity?* Life is opportunity. When does that opportunity end? At death? Death certainly is a radical turning point. When is the final decision given?

Listen to Jesus' words in Mark 9:43–48: "If thy hand cause thee to stumble, cut it off; it is good for thee to enter into that life [that is, the life beyond] maimed, rather than having two hands to go into Gehenna, into the unquenchable fire." Then comes the repetition, with variations of *foot* and *eye*. Then the emphatic "there their worm dieth not, and the fire is not quenched."

Plainly, our Lord teaches here that death is the decision time, the dividing line of opportunity. Life is opportunity; death is the end of opportunity.

Another decisive, explicit passage is the story of the rich man and the poor beggar (Luke 16:19–31). We looked at it fully in "What Can We Know About Others Who Have Died?" Clearly, in this passage, death is settlement time. At death, each case is closed, settled on its merits as they stand at that point. The reward or punishment begins at the turning point of death.

But there is something else. We want to be careful to get all the Scriptures teach, and then strike a balance. There is the passage in 1 Peter, two portions of which come together here. First is this (speaking of Christ): "Being put to death in the flesh, but made alive in the spirit; *in which* he also went and *preached to the spirits in prison,* that aforetime were disobedient, when the long suffering of God waited in the days of Noah," etc. (1 Peter 3:18–20, 4:6).

Note a few things about this passage. These spirits clearly were human spirits who had been disobedient to God's voice during their lives on earth, while Noah was building the ark. They had been swept away in the great Flood. They are said to be "in prison" in the spirit world. This is the only place that phrase is used to describe punishment in the next world (see Jude 6).

It says Jesus went and preached to them. The word *preached* is the word commonly used to mean preaching the Gospel. The inference of this connection is that while Jesus' body lay in the tomb, His spirit went on this gracious errand of mercy. He preached of the Father's love and of His own sacrifice on Calvary. The first preaching of the Calvary message was done by the Calvary Man.

Peter picks up this thread again a few lines farther down: "For *unto this end was the Gospel preached even to the dead,* that they might *be judged* indeed according to men who are still in the flesh, but live according to God in the spirit."

Here is the *purpose* of the preaching. It was preached with a view to the coming judgment. It was to ensure *perfect fairness* in the judging. There would be a full opportunity for a fair, impartial judgment. The inference is that these spirits had not had that full opportunity essential to a fair judgment. In the sweep of the terrible Flood, they had not had their fair chance.

At first thought, it would seem these spirits then did have *another chance* for their salvation after death. But a moment's thinking tells us it was not *another* chance. It apparently was their first opportunity. Our exquisitely fair God was giving them the chance they had not had yet.

Note *this is the only passage* of its kind in the Bible. It is a lonely exception. This is very suggestive and significant. Thousands of passages urge us to make the right choice *now;* just one infers a possible opportunity in the future life.

And the reference is incidental. The main thing Peter is talking about is God's fairness in judgment. Note the teaching principle here. Repetition makes the essential point stand out. The incidental drops practically out of view.

The Bible is an intensely practical Book. It is a model of practical psychology and of applied teaching. It aims continually to make an immediate, practical impression to influence one's decisions and life. It does not tell all the truth. It tells all we need to know in order to make the right decision. Its whole, insistent plea is this: Choose. Choose the only right course. Choose it now, *now*.

God's Fixed Principle of Action

Take another look at the Book. There is *a settled principle underlying God's treatment of humans* who set themselves against Him. He never varies from that principle by so much as a hair width.

It is not *primarily* a principle of punishment, though the fact of punishment is connected to it. It is not an exercise of God's power against these humans. And it is not an *arbitrary* imposing of His will on those unable to resist or escape. Indeed, it is in no way an arbitrary principle.

I use the word *arbitrary* in the positive sense, of course. It may mean "capricious" or "unreasoning." But in law it means "such action or decision as is properly settled upon by the personal judgment or opinion of a judge or tribunal." It stands in contrast to decisions made by certain established rules. Arbitrary action is proper. And God might act in an arbitrary way, with full justice and righteousness.

But the principle that controls God is not arbitrary. It goes *deeper*. It contains more of the heart element, more of the "human" element, the sympathetic element that understands a human's difficulties and surroundings.

It is not just what God *properly might do*. No, the controlling principle is up on the level of strong love. It is what God *prefers to do*. It is the principle that guides *a wise father*.

We think of Matthew 25. In the judgment scene, the King on the throne, who is the Son of man Himself, says to some, "Depart; under a curse," etc. That seems like a properly arbitrary judgment. Yet as we consider it in relation to other passages dealing with the same matter, we see it simply to be the Judge's statement of how the scales swing. The Judge holds the scales steady and true. The human's action tips the scales this way or that. The Judge announces which way the scales tip. It is a pronouncement, not an arbitrary judgment.

The fixed principle that controls God in His dealings with humans is this: *Everyone will be completely free to think and act.* That was the principle in Eden. It *is* the dominating principle as God breathes creative life and spirit into every baby born. It will remain in absolute control in the future. God never has taken away our gift of free choice. He never will.

To appreciate this truth, we must brood over *the character of God*. He is not merely a judge. He is indeed a judge, in the finest sense, but He is more than the standard meaning of that word. He is indeed, as the old phrase says, the moral Ruler of the universe. But with God, the whole thing is on a higher, deeper, more tender "human" level.

It will help in understanding this to recall some of the earlier connotations of the word *father*. We westerners have lost some of the ideals inherent in that word.

The father was the *head* of the family. He ruled. There was no possible exception to his authority.

He was the *priest* of the family. He led its worship. He was God's representative to the family, and the family's representative to God.

He was the *teacher,* instructing, disciplining, and molding.

Mingled inextricably with these concepts was the tenderness of the father for his own child, companionship with the child, devotion to the child, and an intense ambition and pleasure in the child's future. In an emergency, the father made any sacrifice needed for the sake of the child.

That old idea, refined to the utmost, is the one word for God. He is uniquely the Father. He exercises this relationship *creatively* toward everyone, regardless of how we treat God. Of course, He cannot do all He wants for us, unless we let Him.

In contrast with the true meaning of *father* as seen in God, look at the *weak human father*. David let his son Amnon go uncorrected, though Amnon's wrong was abominable. David also let his favorite son Absalom go undisciplined and unpunished. Yet Absalom was a murderer, just as Amnon was an adulterer. So lust and violence—two of the worst demons—were let loose in his kingdom.

David was a wise ruler. But the father in him overcame the king in him. His emotion blurred his judgment. He *knew* full well *as king* how evil his sons' actions were and how disastrous they were to his rule and his kingdom. But emotion dimmed his eye and unsteadied his usually shrewd judgment. The result was that lust and blood ran rampant. He let his weakened fatherly traits dethrone him as king.

That is an illustration of weak fatherhood.

Two Flaming Proclamations

It also will help us to remember the meaning of a phrase like "*the wrath of God.*" It does *not* mean God is angry, in the common sense of that word. It does *not* mean He is "mad at you." Yet many people take it to mean that, especially if they are under the sway of some gifted religious demagogue.

A little thinking into the character of God reveals that the *wrath* of God is His purity blazing out against impurity. It is His fine sense of justice flaming against injustice, His honesty burning against all dishonesty and deception.

His wrath is never against *humans*, except when the human becomes inseparably tangled in the evil he or she has chosen. "The wrath of God is revealed . . .against *all ungodliness* and *unrighteousness* of men" (Romans 1:18).

See what the Scriptures say about the principle controlling God in this matter. On *the very first leaf of the Book,* man is entrusted with the power of free choice and action (Genesis 2:16, 17). His continued good fellowship with God is conditioned on his own choice. He would stay in touch with God if he didn't eat of the tree. He was told not to eat. But it was a matter of choice. He *could* eat, if he wanted.

If he did, the break would follow at once. "Dying, thou shalt die." We see a beginning, a process, and a finished result. The worst result was stated plainly as a guide and a warning. God Himself, man's Companion in the garden, urges the man by His mere presence not to eat of the tree. Separation would result. It would be heartbreaking to God.

There, at the beginning, is the statement of the fundamental principle of free choice.

On the *last page* of the Book is the same thing (Revelation 22:11–15). It is connected with that wonderful picture of the future life in God's presence. But the picture is stained. Then comes the emphasis on this unchangeable principle of God's great love for us, the principle of total free choice.

"He that is set on being unrighteous, let him be wholly free to follow his choice, even here, and do unrighteousness." He faithfully warns, "and it will be with an ever-increasing momentum."

"And he that is set in his choice to go on to the unrestrained depths of lustful passionate indulgence shall be left utterly free to follow his choice, and it will be found that the slant down gets steadily steeper and sharper."

The other side is stated in the same two degrees. "He that is set in his choice to follow only the right and pure and good will be wholly free to follow the bent of his choice, with an ever-increasing ease of movement upward."

"And he that chooses to climb the hill toward the highest peak of personal purity and holiness or wholeness, perfection of character, will have the fullest freedom in following his bent or choice. And he will find too the steepest heights more easily climbed as he goes up."

And when Jesus comes to straighten things out, He will give "to each man according as his choice has been." His blessing is given to those who have insisted on the right choice in spite of difficulties and opposition. These people now do what goes hand in hand with the right choice: They go for cleansing to the blood of the Lamb (Revelation 22:14, with 7:14). "Without" are those whose choice leads them there, and leaves them there.

The two passages are like flaming proclamations at the beginning and end of the Book of God. He does not want humans to ignore or misunderstand this unwavering principle that controls Him, this highest, rarest gift to us: free choice.

In between, the Book is filled with statements and illustrations of the same thing. Open it almost anywhere, at random, and you will find pleadings to choose the right, warnings against persisting in wrong choices, and examples of those who make right and wrong choices.

Here, then, is the unmistakable principle of strong love that controls God in His dealings with humans who are set against His way. It is an unvarying principle. Love never fails. It was that way at the beginning and has remained that way. It always will be that way. Our freedom of action is never interfered with in the slightest.

The Process

It is fascinating to find that *with this principle is a process*. The two go together like a hand in a glove. The principle of love goes with the rare process of love. But notice also the process by which one goes to Hell (my pen sticks with the pain of writing these necessary words).

The human is not sent there or placed there. It is not a case of physical force overcoming resistance and compelling the individual against his or her

will. Human analogies, such as arrest by law en-
forcement officers and enforced imprisonment, fail
to tell this story.

Nor is it by any arbitrary action of God's, though
we might consider such action fair and just. The
process is simply this: *The person is left alone.*
God does nothing. The person is left free to choose.

In the story of the eviction from the Garden of
Eden, it says of God, "So he drove out the man"
(Genesis 3:24). The picture we have had is that of
God forcibly driving Adam and Eve away; they
reluctantly are forced to yield to a power they
cannot withstand. The same word is used by Cain
on the other side of the page: "Behold, thou *hast
driven* me out this day. . .and from thy face shall I
be hid" (Genesis 4:14). We see the same picture as
with Adam and Eve.

But mark what it says a few lines farther down
in describing what actually took place: "And Cain
went out from the presence of Jehovah" (Genesis
4:16). This throws light on the expulsion from
Eden, as well. That last sentence naturally means
no physical force was used, only moral force.

It is almost certain that Adam and Eve were
awed greatly by God's presence and words. Their
consciences were stricken. They were humiliated.
And they went out, as Cain did. What drove them

out was God's love and goodness to them, His purity, combined with their bitter sense of shame and failure and the terrible break they had caused between themselves and God. It is fair to presume their sense of the character of God was so strong that they walked out of their own accord.

This fits perfectly with the striking language Paul uses in that outstanding passage in Romans. There is a terrible indictment of the human race in its sin of going its own way, going against God's way. Paul clearly states God's treatment of them. Three times he says, "*God gave them up*" (Romans 1:24, 26, and 28). God did His best to restrain them. His love, His creative, sustaining care, His pleadings and wooings were lavished on them. Then comes the awful words, "He gave them up." He simply answered their implied, persistent prayer to be left alone. He left them to themselves. The process is clear.

A few years later, writing from Rome to the Ephesians, Paul traces *the steps in the process, on the human side,* by which one goes away from God to his or her doom (Ephesians 4:17–19). He says: "Walk no longer as the outsiders [Gentiles] also walk in the vanity of their mind, being darkened in their understanding, alienated from the life of God, because of the ignorance that is in them, because of the hardening of their heart; who being past feeling gave themselves up to lasciviousness, to work all uncleanness with greediness."

The natural steps in the process partly are reversed here. Paul begins where the outsiders are living the wrong sort of life. Then he traces their steps backward toward their starting point, and adds the climax.

Let's put the events in the order in which they happen naturally. First, there is the "hardening of the heart," the setting of their wills against God. This results in alienation from God. The action automatically cuts them off from God, but the humans, being willfully ignorant, do not realize what they are doing.

Quickly, they are "darkened in their understanding." All mental processes are affected. The moral vision blurs. They call good evil and evil good, darkness light and light darkness, etc. (see Isaiah 5:20). Joined naturally with this is "the vanity in their minds." In failing to get things straight, such humans easily get caught up in their own fanciful ideas.

This, of course, controls their "walk," their daily lives. When they reach this stage, it's only a short step to the sad "past feeling" stage, morally. They give themselves up to unrestrained lust. The last hardened stage is where lust is traded in for dirty gain.

Notice the whole movement is automatic. It is the natural, logical, downward spiral. And this describes things *in this life*. It is like that here. What will it be like *there?* Here, grace still has an influence, even though it is resisted. There, it apparently is shut out.

Jesus' treatment of Judas on the betrayal night sheds light (John 13:21–30). There was the utmost effort to keep Judas *in*. Judas instantly recognized the plain warning as being meant for himself. Then came the tender, personal, loving touch in handing Judas the first morsel from the dish containing the simple evening meal.

Judas hardened his heart against both the warning and the tender pleading. That hardening shut out God and let in someone else. Then Judas, bent on carrying out his purposes, rose and left. He went into the black night.

A Dramatic Illustration

These passages all have to do with the present life —but we are talking about the future life. However, these selections from Scripture reveal God's *habit* in dealing with humans. Basically, this is a question about God. Will God "play fair"?

These verses show how God operates *now*. They also show the *principle* that controls Him in His dealings. We see His steady insistence on humans' freedom of choice, and we see the *process* that works out under that principle. Unless there are specific statements in the Book describing a change of principle and process, we naturally expect this treatment to continue beyond the grave. And there are no contradictory statements.

We turn to the story of Pharaoh in Egypt. God is *dealing in judgment* here. He is correcting long-standing wrongs.

The Hebrews had been wronged severely for several generations. The pharaohs had oppressed them with increasing heartlessness. God had tolerated the pharaohs for a long time, and now it was time to settle. That is what the judgment principle is.

Numerous warnings and pleadings were delivered to Pharaoh before action finally was taken. Then came a carefully arranged series of transactions that brought judgment on Egypt. They grew steadily worse. Between each of them, God gave Pharaoh an opportunity to change.

A significant word is used here. It seems to occur

about nineteen times in a brief space. It is the word *harden,* in varying forms. God says, "I will harden his [Pharaoh's] heart" (Exodus 4:21; 7:3; 14:4, 17). Nine times, in various ways, He is said to harden Pharaoh's heart (Exodus 7:13, 14, 22; 9:12, 35; 10:20, 27; 11:10; 14:8). Five times it says Pharaoh hardened his own heart, or was stubborn (Exodus 8:15, 19, 32; 9:7, 34).

The hardening was and is unnatural, but very common. Humans were created to live in touch with God. If we lose touch, we are out of our native environment, and we do not act as we naturally would. Pharaoh shut *out* God's pleadings and God's presence from his inner heart. He cut himself off from the influence that would have made him act in a true, natural way. As a result, his heart was hardened or heavy. It was set stubbornly. The Bible says he sinned in this very act of hardening his heart against God (Exodus 9:34).

Pharaoh had been doing this a long time. Now the time for decision had come. God lets the Egyptians, the Hebrews, and the rest of the world know of His rejected, scorned power. He withdraws some of His creative touch, His gracious restraint, from Pharaoh. That is all. God does nothing except stop, partly, what He has been doing for Pharaoh.

The judgment includes plagues, pests, disease,

storms, the death of every firstborn Egyptian son, and the drowning of the Egyptian army. In each case, the affliction probably resulted simply from the withdrawal of divine restraint.

In the case of the firstborn dead, nothing the Egyptians could see happened to kill their heirs. All they knew was that the baby or boy or young man was found lying dead.

In the case of the army drowning, the wind blew back the waters. It was a special act of God's power on behalf of His people. He held the waters back; when His people were safe, that power was withdrawn and the law of gravity joined the waters again. The pursuing Egyptians, in their rage, endangered themselves. The danger materialized. The waters swamped them. The *process* was completely natural.

This is more than history. It is teaching. It is a picture of God's patience—the most remarkable divine characteristic in the story. It is a picture of a man's stubborn will outside his native element (God's presence). It is a picture of the principle and process of judgment.

There are certain *apparent* partial exceptions to this law of action. It *seems* to be an arbitrary action by God in destroying the whole human race, except for eight people, in the Flood. It *seems* to be an arbitrary action that wiped out Sodom and the other cities of the plain with a terrific lightning storm.

But we cannot know for sure that they involved arbitrary action. If they did, the action extended simply to the *time* element involved. Sin, left to itself, burns itself out. There seems to have been a *shortening* of the time involved in the natural process. In fact, God patiently may have restrained, preventing the disasters from coming earlier. Then, when His restraint was withdrawn, nature's process worked out naturally—maybe faster, accelerated by the withdrawal of the long restraint.

Notice that God has hung up these and other danger signals in full view. A train I was on passed a large explosives factory. Everywhere around the place I could read, even as we hurried by, warnings in large letters against the use of matches. Some of the railroad company's buildings contained similar warnings because of the buildings' contents.

God's danger signals are in big, bold letters, hung up for all the race to read. The Dead Sea is a warning signal known to all. It is the deepest, ugliest scar on the earth's surface. Neither animal nor vegetable life can exist there. It points to the *fact* of *judgment* against *wrong*.

Closer at hand, nature's laws mercilessly (therefore mercifully) never change. The fire mercilessly burns your hand if you put it in. Instantly you snatch it out. The pain mercifully leads you to keep your whole arm from the flame.

In contrast, man's laws are notoriously loose. As a result, evil spreads. A murderer is acquitted; other murders follow. Failure to uphold the dignity of the law leads to a lowered moral standard. A king or president, loose in personal immorality, always leads the crowd down the same slope.

Nature's laws are merciful because they are so merciless. The warning signals are everywhere.

God's dealing with the human rebel is a process of patient, strong love, and a reluctant withholding of the goodness the rebel is rejecting. It is a process of the rebel's terrible decline.

A Study of Chances

Now we swing back to our starting point. This really is a study of chances. Technically, the matter is not settled at death. It *never* is settled. The way is always open for another chance. That statement is *technically* accurate. So far as the *points* of logic are concerned, the matter never is settled.

But what about *actually?* The average human is concerned only with the *practical.* So now let's discuss the question from the common sense viewpoint. *What are the chances of a person who passes out of this life without taking advantage of his God-given opportunity?* The answer is plain and positive.

A mathematical science is devoted to chances. At least, it is regarded as a science, for financial purposes. Life insurance and assurance companies have experts on chances. The huge volume of business they transact, billions of dollars, is based on the findings of these experts.

These people are called actuaries. Actuaries are skilled in the theory and practice of chances, as applied to human life. They calculate your chances in the most critical, impersonal, dispassionate ways. They have it down to a science, down to a point of knowing certain facts and tendencies. They have worked out the law of chances. In the end, with them, it is purely a matter of money.

Let me say soberly that we have been studying the science of chances here. When you sift through, you find that the last word is not spoken by God. It is spoken by the human. It is completely a matter of choice.

Based on what the Bible tells us of God's character, there is never a time when a truly repentant human cannot turn to Him and find His door wide open. But the chance of a human changing his or her choice is so extremely remote that we can conclude there is no other chance beyond the grave. The matters rests with the person, and the person won't give himself or herself the chance.

The person who does not do today what he or she knows, deep down, should be done is playing the part of a fool. It is a hard word to say, but it is literally true. *This person is playing the part of a fool.* It is a losing game, a lost game. The person still plays, but the game is settled, lost, by the law of chance. That is actually an understatement. The word *fool* does not fully describe this person.

Why do I say that? Read very thoughtfully: It is easier to make the right choice today than it will be tomorrow. That is pure psychology. It is a scientific statement, based on the fixed law of chances.

Let me explain why. It all depends on the part of the human that does the choosing. If you know today, by the inner feel, that you should accept Jesus as your Saviour and accept everything that means, and you do not do it, you are making a decision. You are choosing not to choose.

That act of choosing affects your choosing power. It immediately becomes a bit more set in its way. Like cement, it begins to harden. However slight the hardening may be, it is real. You have a tougher task tomorrow. That inner pull has been offset.

Every tomorrow, the hardening progresses. It grows more unlikely each day that you will make the right choice, because your choosing power gradually is being set the other way. If you do something once, you *can* do it *again*. You are likely to. In fact, you will do it faster and more easily, better and more skillfully.

If that goes on for years, even beyond the grave, it comes to the point where you cannot change. Theoretically you can. As far as God is concerned, the way to Him is open. But in reality, you cannot change. Your choosing power is hardened beyond change. You wouldn't change when you could, and now you cannot. You do not want to.

That is not to say that at this future time when you want to change, you cannot. You still can, as far as God is concerned, but you do not want to. You want to escape the suffering, but you do not want to get into normal touch with God through the crucified Christ.

This is the great, impassable gulf. The rich man of Luke 16 showed no desire to change his choice. There was no change in his attitude toward God or toward his selfish life on earth. The only thing bothering him was the pain he was suffering. He wanted to get rid of that. That was all.

Notice how God limbers up your choosing power so it can reverse itself. It is *not* by some act of judgment, pain, or suffering. All indications are that your choosing power does not tend to soften, but to harden. It is only God's gracious, softening touch that can unlimber that hardened, rusted will. And that touch is being shut out. The human shuts out the one thing that would help make the right choice.

Love Never Fails

So this authoritative Book makes positive statements about the terrible final result for the person who insists on leaving God out, who openly challenges His rule.

The Book has a distinctive way of stating things. It is, of course, an Oriental Book. And it is a popular Book, in the best sense of that word. It is a Book for the common people everywhere.

The Oriental mode of thought and expression is photographic. It shows one picture, stating final, fixed results without giving the process by which the results are reached.

The characteristic Western way is different—cultured, scholarly. It analyzes and dissects the process by which the result is reached. It is more like a motion picture than a still photograph. It tells the story in successive steps.

A distinct touch of divine wisdom and insight is found in this use of the Oriental mode for the Bible. This is the common manner of thought and expression not just in the Oriental world, but among crowds everywhere.

The Book in its rare wisdom expresses the matter in a way that can be understood instantly by anyone in the world. It states the final result. This is the result we have found at the end of our study of the process. It is the result reached by the specialist in the law of probability. It makes a profound impression on the student of the process to see the old Book's rare accuracy and profound human wisdom.

Listen to its simple, positive language: "He that believeth not [or disbelieveth] shall be damned [or condemned]" (Mark 16:16). "He that believeth [or obeyeth] not the Son *shall not see life,* but the *wrath of God abideth on him*" (John 3:36). "These shall go away into *everlasting* [eternal] *punishment*"

(Matthew 25:46). These are authoritative statements, and they are supported fully by the human
law of probabilities.

Is there another chance after death? I thoughtfully repeat the answer: *yes and no*. So far as the
character of God's love is concerned, there is another chance, a chance that seemingly never ends.
So far as a human's decision is concerned, there is
not another chance. And the human's decision is
the determining factor. God leaves the matter to the
human's free choice.

So the last word on the last page of the Bible is
a plea from the Man who died. He cries earnestly,
"He that *will, let* him *take* the water of life freely"
(Revelation 22:17c).

There is a legend of a French mother who loved
her son with a tense, unselfish devotion. But he
was caught in the wildfire of lust. He became fas-
cinated with a beautiful but heartless woman. The
mother clung to and pleaded with the son lovingly.
The evil woman was enraged that she could not
wipe out the mother's influence. In an evil hour,
when her spell was strong, she got the young
man's promise to bring her the heart of his mother.

He kept the promise. Hurrying to his appoint-
ment with the evil charmer, carrying his mother's
heart in a bundle under his arm, he stumbled and

fell. He heard a familiar, tender voice cry, "*O my son, are you hurt?*" The voice bore no reproach, only undying, self-sacrificing love.

It is only a legend—but true to life. The son could kill his mother, but he could not kill her love or shut out her voice. The mother's love is the greatest human love. The heartfelt love of a mother comes nearest to God's heart.

God suffers when any creative child of His suffers. He suffers more when someone goes to Hell than the human suffers. But He will not rob the person of free choice.

God's love never fails. It cannot. It will not.

Inspirational Library

Beautiful purse/pocket size editions of Christian classics bound in flexible leatherette. These books make thoughtful gifts for everyone on your list, including yourself!

The Bible Promise Book   Over 1000 promises from God's Word arranged by topic. What does the Bible promise about matters like: Anger, Illness, Jealousy, Love, Money, Old Age, and Mercy? Find out in this book!
Flexible Leatherette $3.97

Daily Light   One of the most popular daily devotionals with readings for both morning and evening.
Flexible Leatherette $4.97

Wisdom from the Bible   Daily thoughts from Proverbs which communicate truths about ourselves and the world around us.
Flexible Leatherette $4.97

My Daily Prayer Journal   Each page is dated and features a Scripture verse and ample room for you to record your thoughts, prayers, and praises. One page for each day of the year.
Flexible Leatherette $4.97